D1400321

THEY FOLLOWED HIS CALL

Vocation and Asceticism

ADRIENNE VON SPEYR

THEY FOLLOWED HIS CALL

Vocation and Asceticism

TRANSLATED BY
ERASMO LEIVA-MERIKAKIS

IGNATIUS PRESS   SAN FRANCISCO

Title of the German original:
Sie Folgten Seinem Ruf
© 1955, Johannes Verlag, Einsiedeln
First U.S. edition, © 1979, Society of St. Paul

Cover by Victoria Hoke Lane

With ecclesiastical approval
Revised edition, © 1986, Ignatius Press, San Francisco
All rights reserved
ISBN 0-89870-100-7
Library of Congress catalogue number 86-80294
Printed in the United States of America

CONTENTS

FOREWORD

This little book can be understood only if we go behind
the worn facade of the words *ascesis* and *ascetic* and
penetrate those Christian sources that first made men
put themselves wholly and undividedly at the service
of God's Word and follow his lead. We will then not
mind it if, especially in its first part, the book understands "ascetical life" to be a life called to undivided
service, a life, therefore, shaped by the three evangelical
counsels. At first, the book accompanies the young
person very seriously and even maternally through the
difficult time that leads from the call's awakening in the
soul to the great Decision and its realization. Each phase
has its particular form of *ascesis,* always understanding
the term here in the Christian sense of a reality that
makes a claim on the total existence of a believing
person and that derives wholly from God's calling Word,
never as the sum of particular "works" or "achievements",
although the call to ascetical life is always also a call to
action.

The sense of a life in the evangelical counsels is
always to lead one out more and more, out of the
private and personal and into the total ecclesial reality.
The three counsels are here considered under the per-
spective of this opening out. With Chapter VIII we
arrive at the ascetical demand that God's calling Word
makes of all Christians, even those living in the world—a
demand that is one with the ascesis of ecclesial existence.

The renunciation involved in hearing the Word correctly; the renunciation to which this Word educates every believer; the renunciation that is necessarily contained in every reception of a sacrament; the renunciation implied in the simple love of one's neighbor. All of these renunciations are not negations but mysteries of the highest joy and liberation—the freedom to participate in the eternal truth and reality—God's own Love, which in the Redemption pours itself out so prodigally.

The way which Adrienne von Speyr here undertakes anew is a way that seeks to convince through its totality. Whoever keeps his gaze on the Whole, the overpowering Whole, can no longer hold himself back on account of some particular thing. Christianity's Whole gives such happiness that, because of it, even the hardships of asceticism can be demanded. Only because he gives everything, a divine Everything, does Christ demand and expect from the believer his small, human everything. The book is meant to be read and understood in the sense of this totality.

Hans Urs von Balthasar

INTRODUCTION:
On the Life of Adrienne von Speyr

Before—and even after—reading *They Followed His Call,* readers will be interested to know something about the life of Adrienne von Speyr (1902–1967), a remarkable European woman of our times: wife, mother, physician and, above all, a contemplative theologian of the greatest precision, intensity and spiritual depth.

Adrienne was born on September 20, 1902, in the city of La Chaux-de-Fonds, Switzerland, the second daughter of a surgeon. From early childhood, Adrienne loved to pray to God and experienced the guidance of what she took to be an angel. She accompanied her father on visits to the sick and was even able to comfort mental patients in an asylum run by her uncle.

From an early age, she herself wanted to become a doctor, a plan thwarted for many years by her mother's conviction that women should not be doctors. A brilliant girl, she persevered in her studies in spite of serious illnesses predicted to be fatal and the necessity of supporting herself by means of long hours of tutoring. During this time she was experiencing interior and exterior visions of Mary, the angels and the saints, especially of Saint Ignatius of Loyola. Certainly any student of Catholic feminine spirituality will recognize the profound relationship between perseverance in tasks outside the accepted social structure and the conviction of a call to service inspired not merely by human inclination but by a leading of the Holy Spirit.

In 1927 Adrienne married Emil Dürr, a widower with two children, and dean of the department of history at the University of Basel. In 1936, two years after his sudden death, she remarried. Her second husband was Werner Kaegi, then chairman of the same history department.

In spite of the prejudices against Catholicism prevalent in her milieu, Adrienne von Speyr had always been attracted to the spirituality of the Catholic Church. In 1940 she began instructions in the faith under the direction of Hans Urs von Balthasar, the renowned Swiss theologian. Of this period of Adrienne's life, von Balthasar gives a description which could also be applied to the conversion experience of many others:

> I found that while she did not already simply know the things I told her, she at once recognized them as valid and true. For thirty-eight years she sought for them with all her might, had groped her way toward them in darkness, had prayed ceaselessly, so that the outline of Catholic truth was, as it were, hollowed out in her like the impress of a mold. It needed only a brief indication so that when she grasped a point, it became whole within her, she said her "Yes!" to it with all her heart and in almost boundless joy.[1]

She was baptized on the feast of All Saints in 1940. At this time she was working full time as a doctor, seeing as many as sixty to eighty patients a day. In spite

[1] Hans Urs von Balthasar, *Erster Blick auf Adrienne von Speyr*, p. 10.

of their number her personal response to each patient was a fruit of her deep compassion for the physical and mental suffering of others. She was able to save thousands of babies from abortion. Most of her practice was among the poor, whom she treated free of charge. What a stirring example of how Christians can answer the call of Christ by means of their professional commitments!

During this period she was receiving extraordinary graces in prayer, reaching an apex at Passiontide and finally leading to the stigmata. She prayed that these external signs would be hidden from all but her confessor, to whom she dictated her visions.

Knowing something about these graces helps us to understand the atmosphere of infused contemplation characterizing her writing. In our era, where introspective reflection has been cultivated often to the point of faddishness, we are stunned to read spiritual books of such intensity which simply transmit something seen as true, without the slightest trace of subjective embellishment. This is similar to the shock of hearing Gregorian chant after years of immersion in Romantic music. Finally, as we allow ourselves to be purified, we realize that the most passionate beauty comes not from within ourselves but exists in God himself, to whom we are invited to respond at least with all our hearts and to let the bonfire of our desperate human loves become the still, intense flame of the Marian assent of which Adrienne writes so movingly.

To return to the story of Adrienne's life: we find her for the last twenty years of her life accepting the heavy physical crosses of diabetes and arthritis. Unable to continue her medical practice, she would spend most of her night in prayer, while during the day she would embroider, knit for the poor and immerse herself in the sufferings of contemporary man by means of reading novels of the times.

It will probably be thought, from this description, that Adrienne was a rather solemn person. On the contrary, von Balthasar describes her as an extremely joyful woman with a lovely sense of humor and child-like delight in every aspect of life.

In many ways, the culmination of the spiritual friend-ship of Adrienne von Speyr and Hans Urs von Balthasar, her confessor, was the founding of a secular institute, a form of the life of vowed consecration in which lay people and priests take the evangelical vows while devot-ing themselves to the sanctification of the world. Many of Adrienne's spiritual commentaries on the Gospels were written for this community. *They Followed His Call* is but one example of the more than sixty volumes which she dictated to Father von Balthasar.

During her last ten years, Adrienne von Speyr suffered excruciating physical pain with great courage, finally unable to work or to see. Among her final words before her death at the age of sixty-five on September 17, 1967, were these:

"How beautiful it is to die."[2]

Ronda Chervin

[2] Ibid., p. 41.

I

THE ANSWER TO GOD'S CALL

A call is always from the Lord. He knows all the world's roads and the needs of all engaged upon them. He continues to work redemption by calling persons to help him in this task. That they should help, however, is not what first becomes apparent from the call.

There are many who hear God's call over and over again without taking it seriously. They have an exact idea of what God does in order to find workers for his vineyard. They can develop theories about the answers of those called and they know precisely what the minimum is that a person can offer God. They also know the maximum. But in all this they close their hearts, as if none of it concerned them personally, as if their role were only to be observers, or at best, witnesses. They amuse themselves speculating who could be meant, or how this or that one ought to have answered. They would even like to give their dear God advice as to how to make his call even more emphatic and enticing, how to make his language more understandable. Only they themselves do not hear.

God calls and man has only to listen. The ear which God the Father has given man is capable of receiving the call that goes out from God. But it seems that it is always a long road from the ear to the will and to love.

God calls in Scripture, God calls in sermons, God also calls in every prayer. There is no truly prayed prayer in which his call does not resound. Whether it is the Our Father or the Hail Mary or prayer that one composes: God's voice is always in the background. No prayer can be uttered without man's realizing that, in it, God is calling. If I can pray and believe, hope and love, it is only because God calls, because his voice cannot grow mute, because God wants to say something special to each individual person. And he never grows tired from always repeating the ancient statement, from turning to men through all the centuries and informing them of his own concerns, of his will that they should follow him. It was already the most extreme form of God's call that his Son became Man, small and naked and helpless, and that he lived among us as One among the countless millions. He humiliated himself so profoundly in order to show how great God's concerns are, in order to demonstrate how urgent an answer to God is and how very little he desires to remain alone. He bore everything—even the Cross—in solitude. But his alone-ness and forsakenness witness only more loudly to his call. They are an expression of the way his love is directed towards men. This is not only a love that *bears,* but a love that *needs;* not only a love that squanders itself, but a love that cannot exist without the other squandering himself.

God calls even where men sleep. On the Mount of Olives, the Son calls his sleeping disciples. He calls them in such a way that, even though they overhear his

call, they nevertheless know darkly that it rings on.
The Son then prays to the Father in his aloneness, and
yet he became Man in order to go to the Father together
with us. He always lets us partake in his prayer and in
every word he speaks. We are called even to where he is
alone with the Father. He never lays us down like a
burden; we are never too much for him. And in his
word to the Father, he anticipates our answer to him: he
assumes that we will give an answer. He does not want
to stand before the Father on the Mount of Olives as a
disappointed man. His prayer is always a banquet and
we are always the guests.

The sleeping disciples had once answered. They had
taken up their tasks and, with that, they seemed to have
done enough. Their discipleship is assured. Why should
they now again be called, or even themselves become
callers along with the Lord? They sleep; but they should
be watching. . . . To be watchful, to be available, to be
able to wait, but also to have a readiness that can
suddenly become action: all of these are prerequisites
for perceiving the call. No one who has ever answered
has answered perfectly or given the extreme, the last
thing he has left to give. For no one can presume that
his actions suffice, that the call no longer concerns him,
that he has achieved what was expected.

The call is not only an invitation, but at the same
time a word of encouragement, of light, love, something that becomes fruitful in the person himself, something that comes to life in letting itself be perceived and
that offers help and spurs the hearer on. The Lord takes

his call back to himself in the answer of a person that satisfies him. No sooner has the answer reached the Lord, however, than he gives it back in the form of a new call.

The call reaches persons in their youth and also older persons. But the "late-called" are mostly those with whom the Lord's patience has persevered for so long that they have at last heard. If he closely examines his life, such a person will see that he owes his vocation to God's long suffering. But the one who is called and answers in his youth does not for that reason have an easier time of it, since he is called to more, to a longer season of listening and answering. He cannot, because he gives himself, guarantee that he will remain faithful nor can he set any bounds to his faithfulness and endurance. He cannot say: "this far and no further!" That would be a self-willed limitation of his answer to a particular time and space. In order to remain alive in a person, God's call knows only eternity as a time and infinity as a space. And where infinity and eternity are involved man can mark off for his stance no firmly established place. As soon as he has heard himself being called, he must persevere precisely in the attitude of one called. God himself takes his education in hand; no time is set in advance as the period for his testing. In every situation he will have to change, will have to answer differently, and for this reason his readiness may, in no connection, become fixated. Mary spoke her Yes of consent in this way: as one who intends to remain permanently in a Yes-attitude, even when the demands change, even when disappointments and setbacks come. The Yes continues as a long, reverberating echo and is constantly repeated. And if a person no longer finds in himself the strength for such a Yes, even though he has remained faithful, God gives it to him along with his call, perhaps in a humbling of the person, who now knows that even his Yes has been taken over by God; perhaps, too, in a simple taking over of the answer, unknown even to the person. God behaves like a master who is sure of his servant. He counts on him today because he could count on him yesterday. He pays no heed to the fact that the servant's fidelity has today broken down, that today the believer's Yes no longer has any force, that it comes with hesitation, has perhaps become inaudible. God pays no heed to any of this because he has also taken this upon himself, because God never tires, and vouches for the limitless, extensive and ever wider quality not only of the call, but also of the answer.

Children often think, "Once I grow up, I'll make decisions, take up tasks, have a freedom I now lack." They think, "The bigger you get, the bigger the world also becomes." But when the adolescent hears God's voice, it seems as if he were suddenly put back in the days of his childhood. The childhood he now experiences, however, and which he perhaps adorns with memories of things once experienced, does not correspond to his previous childhood. It is a condition of again being underage, which can go beyond itself only through the freedom of the answer.

The one called hears the Voice as just such an individual. It came to *him* and not to anyone around him. It
meant *him*. It encountered him just as he was, with both
his good and his bad sides, with his past and his present.
Once the call becomes a certainty for him, grace becomes
palpable. He feels impelled to spend himself, being
thankful, and yet he also feels frightened in the face of
the new vocation. Since he belongs to the Church as
one called, he feels an obligation to talk about it with
his confessor. Possibly it was the Church which externally
mediated the call: it might have been heard in a sermon,
in confession, at communion or perhaps in a prayer
spoken outside church and the context of the liturgy.
The searching soul has turned to God and asked a word
from him, and it received it. But even then the same
holds. As soon as the call resounds, there takes place a
sort of veiling of the personality. One is not called as a
private person; rather something in the Church is called
up in the person which awakens to a new liveliness. The
Church thus has a claim on him which he must fulfill. If
he is called to the priesthood or to an order, the one
called will only seldom find his way alone to the door
of the seminary or novitiate. He will have to take up
correspondence, if only to receive the needed recom-
mendations and the testimonies concerning his previous life, a life that in retrospect does not even to him
appear to be the life of one called. The priest to whom
he turns will introduce his entire existence as one called
into a frame of reference in which he will at first appear
as a stranger to himself, hearing, perhaps, of the road

followed by saints or other persons who heard a similar voice under similar circumstances. Long before it is decided to what community he will belong or whether he should become a priest or a lay brother he will receive a sense of solidarity with persons that until now had been indifferent to him. And what he had hitherto regarded as his most personal possession, his unique experiences, his causes for enthusiasm and joy, will now descend into a certain anonymity. He has already been integrated before he knows *into what.* And when he confesses from now on, he does it as one called. His errors no longer belong to him alone and are no longer forgiven him alone; they are signs of a disorder which his new life-situation cannot tolerate. His responsibility has become much greater, not on account of what he is, but on account of the surrender of himself about to take place: the seminary, the order, his new vocation cannot use him if he is like *that!* Like John the Baptist, he "must decrease". The concern for the salvation of his own soul, his ideal of perfection, his striving after virtue have all become alien to him. He is taking up the striving of a new life. His personal views about all of this and about the ways of implementing it no longer count. What counts are the views that have been preserved in the Church that took form long before he gave his consent and long before he existed. The Church accepts his consent, to be sure, with a gratitude that may not always be evident to him, but even more tangibly according to an already-established order of law to which he must now give himself. Here, for the first time in his new life, he collides with the reality of asceticism. If he is truly called, the order will accept him, but it will also expect of him an about-face more radical than any personal conversion. All sorts of unknown and unfamiliar things now impose themselves on him with disorienting sobriety. It seems to him as if he has set out on an expedition into a hitherto closed territory in the Church which has always gotten along without him as it now does *with* him and where he must now silently "fit in". What he brings with him—his personality, his experiences, his past life—has lost its character of inalienable possession and has somehow become indifferent. Everything has gained a share in an objectivity unknown to him until now. He experiences an unsuspected sacramental atmosphere within the Church. In personal confession, in private communion, in being with others—everywhere—the Church now has a right to express itself through him. And where should the Church ultimately not have that right when a Christian is involved who knows himself to be called? Everything is animated by a new necessity which he can experience only in the interior of his consent. This consent opens up to him a world which he possibly did not even wish to know. But, with his consent, there is no going back.

Whoever experiences these things ought not to give expression to this strangeness or to the fact that he expected things to be otherwise; this would only weaken the power of the call he has received, as well as the urgency of his answer. He must accept it as it offers itself, with the same matter-of-factness and apparent indifference with which he takes his first meal in the new community. He will do this perhaps very consciously by committing things to memory, or perhaps only half-consciously, making an effort not to stand out by his actions and attitudes, and trying to fit in exteriorly even before he can keep up interiorly. It is of no use to think back or to cling to the ideas one had associated with entering. It is simply different than had been expected; not only new, but strange, even cold. Perhaps he feels unwanted; or at any rate like one to whom neither the Church nor the order are about to make any concessions. And yet, the consent continues to flow. The call had meant him and no other. The de-personalization that had begun already by the fact of communicating the call to the confessor or a religious or whomever, constitutes a necessary first phase, a beginning. It is a sign that not only God, but also the Church has begun to take him in earnest. There will still be many phases of this voluntary self-depersonalization. Through rule, the occupation and daily life in a Church manifests itself to him as if for the first time. The consent of the one called belongs, furthermore, to the Church's tradition; it becomes integrated with the Son's consent to the Father, the Mother's consent to the angel and with those called in both the Old and New Testaments. Not only is there a theology of consent, but also an immediate ecclesial effect brought about by the integration of the newly called into the community of all who say Yes. There is a sum of all consents which radiates a certain energy and which takes each consent spoken anew and draws it into itself. The one who says Yes senses something of this. He feels himself grasped by a towering reality which works on him and refashions him until he is at last usable for the Church—not without his assent; indeed according to his intentions. The extent of the transformation, the direction in which he moves, has very little left to do with his person any more. He has only to limp along, full of gratitude, since he has entered not the harsh impartiality of a worldly school, but the source of unheard-of graces, whose essence seems to consist in surpassing his understanding. He stands in the midst of the drizzle and yet cannot feel it. He has already been doused in such a way that the new rain is not perceptible to him, and he does not even have the certainty of being where he should be. The certainty lay in the Yes. Now it is as if this certainty had returned to the origin of all Yeses in order to be poured out again to those whom the Lord, along with the Church, will call tomorrow or in the future.

N B

II

THE SACRIFICES OF THE DECISION

The young person who thinks he is perceiving a call from God can, indeed, experience a mysterious joy. But he cannot conceive of his present and past life as being united with the call, as being a life within the call. He has an idea about himself; he knows his mistakes and somehow also his gifts and also his desires for life; he sees what he has accomplished up to today and how much more remains to be done—all of it very soberly. Everywhere he clashes with his limitations. He partly lives in a world of daydreams and fantasy, where things have other names and words other sounds. There he "sets his existence aright", leaving outside what could become unpleasant and lending the one he loves a heightened presence and significance. He lends greater life, too, to those things about himself he would like to change, perhaps even beginning to believe, out of an excess of imagination, that it is already so today. . . .

When God's call really sounds, however, all previous judgments and valuations are bracketed, the sober ones as well as the fantastic. The call is the absolute fact, the unvitiated objectivity. It is the voice of God that addresses itself to a particular person. Through this call the person, the addressee, becomes who he is, and he enters the only light that truly illumines him. All that is positive, all that is negative about him becomes manifest and the call, in its perfection and impartiality, begins to have its effects at once. Dreams, unrealities and imaginings fall away like a garment that one no longer needs and which no longer fits.

Whether the person says Yes immediately and proceeds to realize his call, or whether external obstacles oppose themselves to the immediate forsaking of all things and the person must, for the time being, live in a preliminary time of transition: whatever the case, the consent has an immediate effect, since God's call is an immediate reality. The call strips him of all that is superficial, but it burdens him heavily with new things that begin to transform him and his life in the direction of his choice.

Never again will change in him occur according to the pattern of his dreams and desires, rather always in the direction marked by the call and its sober effects. It could be that already now, in the time remaining before admittance, a certain instruction takes place, introducing the person to the kind of life he will later find in an order or seminary and already forming him for what is to come. But it could equally happen that the kind of effect that the person undergoes corresponds to no specific order or spiritual direction, but involves solely God's naked working in the soul. Whatever God rejects is excluded; whatever he welcomes is striven after. The person becomes something other than what he was. This change is primarily interior, hidden; it chiefly concerns his prayer, his interior life, his outlook on the world and things in it. He must think about certain details in an almost petty way: whether this or that is still appropriate or feasible. Other things he can either reject or accept generously. In this way, a strong change can begin even in his external way of life which distinguishes him from his surroundings, but this is always in keeping with the soberness of his call. In the event the person wanted to accompany his consent with endless "outpourings of the heart" and to continue what had perhaps begun austerely in an extravagant, sentimental or ostentatious way, it would be certain that the call had not remained a living reality in him. This would, of course, say nothing about the genuineness of the original call, but it would give reason for the greatest fears concerning the genuineness of the answer and of his present dialogue with God. God's genuine call would have been mixed with man's ungenuine response in such a way that the former was choked. Man is called by God in freedom. God humbles himself as a caller so deeply that a person can hear and understand him in a human way and, therefore, also possesses the ability not to hear God and to turn away. A plant that is overrun with parasites ends up not absorbing any air or water or soil, because the foreign growth snatches everything for itself. The one called and the one helping him as advisor through this time of transition must, therefore, devote time and attention to the call, taking care that it thrives. But this thriving can occur only at the cost of the self-will of the one called. He has answered freely; whether he now remains free in the answer depends on him. The increased freedom of the call to which he has said Yes now has every privilege in him and must keep it. The call destroys whatever is incompatible with it and fosters whatever is favorable to it without worrying about the person's petty attachments and the plans he has already made.

The strengthening of the call in a person has the immediate result that each of God's words resounds more loudly. The whole of Scripture now becomes a living reality for him: the Word becomes flesh in him. What until now seemed to him to be a more or less dry Word on paper—in spite of his assenting to it—a not totally binding Word, now becomes to him more living than himself, following from his vocation. One can often see immediately to which order certain older religious belong, since the spirit of their community has thoroughly embodied itself in them, in their character and bearing, their speech and attitudes. Something of this "embodiment" has to commence at once after the consent, even though it will become complete only slowly and organically. The person must accept being "stamped" in a certain way by the Spirit, even though he himself may not be able to determine clearly what this Spirit consists of. He has to be open, like a blind man, to whatever God considers necessary to effect in him.

It thus becomes apparent that many things happen in a totally unexpected manner. The person freely gives back to God what until now he had considered to be his inviolate privilege. Before his consent, such a loss would have been painfully felt, but now it counts not at all. Other things that earlier had apparently meant nothing to him now become the most difficult, things that he can hardly give, that strain and consume his energies and that seem to put gall in his coming life and even in his present moment. Again and again, we affirm that we know that God has from all eternity predetermined our road, and we insist that we want to walk in those predetermined paths. But when things become serious, when God's call, when God's will becomes fully visible in his Word as our absolute, eternal life, then the one called can find it most difficult. He must learn to look on the unexpected as the only possible thing and on what God in his freedom gives him as the One Thing Necessary. It means nothing for him to surrender, for him to give himself away time and again, if in so doing he ignores the particular, slow and tough aspects of God's will. Surrender must be carried out by combining generosity with an exactness that is attentive to the smallest details. This attitude is not "built-in" in ourselves; it must be derived as the answer patterned on God's demands. The "Not my will, but yours, be done" becomes evident in the answer from the beginning, but less in man's answer to God than in the answer which God for his part gives to the answering person. This answer of God is always a new, active and living demand. But this activity and liveliness is very different from what man imagines. The reality is at once harder and softer because it is life. And, because it derives from God's own life, this reality can neither be measured nor assigned to a particular place nor predetermined. The dialogue of God the Father with the Son who remains on earth is perhaps the most living reality one could ever conceive of, and out of this most living reality is created God's call to man.

And yet many subjective elements play a role in the choice of a state of life. One must not only come to terms with oneself, but with an entire milieu that includes the Church. The asceticism of the one called, which previously had seemed asceticism only with regard to the naked call, now must actively incorporate his whole concrete environment.

The small child has a very vague idea of states in the Church. He sees the difference between his father and a priest, his mother and a nun, who perhaps is his teacher. He exchanges a word now and then with members of the clergy or the religious state, a word that establishes a contact, a meeting, a relationship from which something endearing emanates. But then the priest disappears into his rectory, the sister into her convent, and the child finds himself again in the usual world of home and buddies. The admonitions he receives from priest and nun—to be good, to carry out his tasks with diligence and not to get into fights—are all directed to the child's world in which he lives. They allow him little participation in the world of those called to the religious life; they somehow emphasize the difference between the two worlds; and yet they are the right advice, an advice that strengthens him and makes him develop in his own world.

If a call then goes out to this young person and he feels he must enter the world of persons with a vocation, he must subject his whole personal world to a new trial. In so doing, a conflict of duties can easily occur. Perhaps the person involved is a leader of a youth group in the parish. He considers this a serious task. Or perhaps his obligations concern his parents, his younger brothers and sisters or his friends. These are all tasks of the Christian apostolate in one's environment, tasks that have been precisely inspired and entrusted to him by his spiritual mentors and which are the normal continuation of the manner in which they had earlier initiated the child into the sphere of duty. And now God's call demands that the youth leave all of this aside. Even things which have been presented and entrusted to him as duties and activities of the most positive nature by the Church's representatives themselves! Since he is only a human being, a great portion of his thoughts remain purely human. Interest for his convenience, his reputation, for acting correctly, is laid on the scales and, perhaps for the first time, really is made to count. He sees a humanly prescribed way before him that could bring him honor. He is perhaps still too young to realize the questionableness of plans that are made single-handedly by an individual. In order to find a counter-balance against God's call, he will cling to every possible thing—to every plausible word he is told that warns him and counsels him to be sober. He will probably make it all into an omen, a sign that he was, in fact, about to commit a stupidly rash action.

It could be that those representatives of the Church, who know the possibility of a call and talk about it in theory, are the same who, in the concrete, are an obstacle to the call by all the advice they have given the young person both as a child and as an adolescent. By judgments and emphases which are all too final, narrow and categorical about the family, love of neighbor, apostolate in the parish and in one's secular profession, they have so cluttered the field of vision that one can no longer see that God is all and that against his call there can be no pretexts. The voice must be given so much room for play that all argumentation grows silent before it, if not immediately, then with time. Every human decision must be made to foster the divine decidedness of that voice which, against each instance of human wisdom, provides in advance the most excellent of all wisdom. Although the Gospels first relate how the apostles straightaway forsook everything to follow the Lord and only later speak of the difficulties of their chosen road, we cannot conclude from this that the first step was easy for them. The following of Christ always represents a painful break in life. The renunciation is real but the import of the call outweighs everything else. Whoever is called must do everything in order to remain within reach of the voice. If once the voice grows silent, everything is lost. The one called would rather lose everything than have the voice become muted. The voice *effects* discipleship. It is at the same time the Yes and the inability to say No. The idea of a life without this voice appears as an unbearable solitude.

And so, one must follow: who knows whether the voice will ever let itself be heard again?

The muting of the voice is such a frightening event and it so unsettles the person that whoever has said No or tried to put God off, postponing a decision, is a permanently marked man. He is and remains recognizable. He has pushed aside *the* experience of his life. In the future he remains embittered, dissatisfied, sarcastic and fault-finding, and he never grows tired of exposing his reasons, just concealing a sense of "knowing better" and trying to prove the impossibility of discipleship. But he is marked in advance; his words are superfluous. The No impresses itself and remains, and it is at times more capable of transforming a person's spiritual physiognomy more deeply than the Yes would have done. And if the young, inexperienced person had enough experience, his consent could have been supported also with negative reasons—namely, not to become like those who refuse themselves to God—and thus he would avoid spoiling with this No his unique earthly life once and for all in such a way that he can neither become the person he intended to be nor the one God meant for him to be. The consenter knows that much struggle awaits him. He will not always have joy; hours of doubt will overfall him; his mistakes and weaknesses will not abandon him. He will be in the danger of increasing the multitude of the lukewarm. He does not have the feeling that the monastery, seminary or community receiving him is gaining much. He is a questionable gift with which they will be able to do less than with most of the others who could have applied. He, nevertheless, has no choice, since God has precisely pointed to him. God wants him, and God, therefore, provides the voucher for him. If God gives him the strength to consent, he can also give him the strength to persevere in letting himself be changed. His awareness that this strength is being bestowed by God allows him to draw the line of demarcation and to sacrifice whatever is demanded. He derives the strength to avoid always computing in a petty way the value of each individual thing he must give up. Rather, he learns to appreciate rightly the value of things from the one great gift he makes. For him, they are gifts which he is allowed to give away. In this way, he will be able to renounce things in order to remain in the domain of God's voice. His place is not alongside the voice, nor in the space of an echo, but right in the middle of the voice, where the Word is a living thing and has the name of God.

III

THE TIME OF CHOICE

Surrender to the Lord—perfect, unconditional surrender
—is an ascetical deed that contains in itself, or at least
should contain in itself, everything having to do with
the Lord's plans for a person. And so, the first quality of
this deed is readiness, an open readiness that is not
always trying to calculate what for us is possible, easily
possible, then just possible and finally wholly impossible.
This readiness has an openness about it that has the
courage of leaving to the Lord what is his. The time
when a person hears God's call and has to decide can in
no way be the time of trying out all possible ascetical
exercises or acts of penance, whether according to a
fixed program or arbitrarily, following the inspiration
of the moment. It is not the time to find out how far
one can go in fasting, in watching in long prayer vigils
or in mortifications. One's readiness should leave everything to the openness of the spirit, as well as that of the
body and of time, and this readiness is the foundation
of all asceticism. It cannot be a lukewarm readiness, but
a living one, no *laissez-faire,* but a being watchful, a
receptivity, and also a thankfulness that the Lord has
called. And his thankfulness should already be present
even when this call has not gained clear contours. One
doesn't know yet the sense of God's call or to what one

is being called, but one *does* know that God is speaking, that his Word has become perceivable. Already this fact should spur a person on to an ultimate readiness to will what God wills—whether the content of this will is revealed or not—in an anticipating zealous love. It is love that envelops every form of asceticism with the force and manifestness of a blazing fire that encloses God's territory and builds a burning wall through which no person can any longer penetrate, since it is God who himself has kindled the fire and who *is* the fire. And, because this wall is made of fire, it is also a purifying, exterminating element. That which is superfluous is excised and the essential is chiseled to a clean shape. In this process, a person may experience his existence in a new way, from the bottom up. Because of God, revaluations may now take place that are fundamental for all future life. The essential is separated from the unimportant in a manner that is God's and which a person would never have attained on his own. The asceticism of readiness certainly also implies increased prayer, an intensified seeking after God, a sharpened attentiveness to his Word, but all of it, not in the form of a training, but following the promptings of love. As soon as things become stiff, shut off, and are done out of habit, we no longer have to do with the asceticism of the time of choice.

The experiences of the time of choice are comparable to those of a young mother who, before marriage, had only a theoretical knowledge of how to care for an infant. And now suddenly she is responsible for her living child's most diverse needs. Through his presence

God shows what he needs, asks for and expects. He creates new times and divisions in a day's work, new tools, too, and qualities. A person attempts to reciprocate God's new wishes and designs as best as he can. For the most part, this will mean valuing one's self and one's things less highly, leaving everything to God in ever greater measure, until we can perhaps say that we have totally forgotten about ourselves and find all meaning in God. It will mean standing so much on God's side that what commonly, humanly speaking, would be considered to be penance, expiation, a burdensome life, now simply bears the name of *love*. A person will now rejoice when God asks him for this or that. Sacrifice will no longer seem to be a deprivation but a gift that God accepts, a gift that he prepares, even as he asks for it, because with his question he already is bestowing an answer on the person. In everyday life, however, this self-surrender implies no passivity. On the contrary, it implies that one will carry everything out as well as possible in order to keep half-achievements and an imprudent activism from being obstacles to total obedience. Surrender will keep his relationship to God free from the dross of a bad conscience.

During this time, a person will have to cut himself off from many things, but he may not regard with contempt what he has left behind. He has made his decision out of love for God, but also for the world. The world is not to be hated; it is to be loved so much that one offers it to God and makes of it and of one's involvement in it a sacrificial gift that God desires. As in the case of

Thérèse of Lisieux, it could be that the sacrifice that God asks for consists of nothing but negligible acts of self-denial.

A person could be ready, as far as he was concerned, to renounce important things to which he had hitherto clung; but God's wishes could, on the contrary, demand that he retain them, and the person comes to discern God's will in this retainment and perseverance. This will change his relationship to these cherished things. He will now love them because God incites him to it and in this way envelop in a Christian love what he had once loved in a worldly way. He will also be ready always to offer these things to God again, but not through petty insisting and pressuring as if he wanted to substitute God's true will with another self-made will, and not in an attitude of "knowing better than God", as if he had always to be proving his readiness through renunciations God now wants to know nothing about.

Everything has to proceed with the naturalness of the children of God and with the joy and gratitude of the call. No artificial program is here involved, no program at all, in fact, but only love and simplicity: joy in prayer, joy in everything through which God reveals himself, joy in his world and in his heaven, joy in the transitoriness of time as being an expression of eternity. For how should a person ever know what eternal time is if God did not give him, in transitoriness, a foretaste of eternity?

Whoever knows himself to be called by God may no

longer quarrel with God concerning the call. He should manage to remain simple and childlike in his consent. Childlike, because God is the Father of those he calls, and the Father/child relationship is continually exemplified both in the orders and in the priesthood through obedience. Childlikeness can assume different forms according to the order chosen, just as obedience adapts itself to the particular rule of an order. But childlikeness it must nevertheless be, and therefore also simplicity, a looking away from one's self in order to have one's glance free for God. The small everyday problems concerning state in life and faith, which up to now concerned the person, suddenly lose their urgency. The important thing now is to listen to God's Word, to the dialogue between Father and Son, so as to be receptive for the sonship destined for those called to the discipleship of the Lord.

Prayer should leave its stamp on a person's total attitude toward life, and it should make the one called into a kind person, a loving person who infects others with his love. They ought not only to feel loved; the question itself of love should awaken in them: "What is the nature of a love that can transform that person in such a way? How could I myself acquire such a love? How did he ever come upon it?" Such questions concerning love could be roads to God. Everything about the one called should point to God and not to himself. His apostolate will be much less one of word than one of deed, but more in the sense of "letting happen" than of actively intervening. Whenever a word is necessary he will say it, but he will not preach or hold talks. He will simply attempt to let his happiness shine through. Even though he is interiorly detached from his previous life, this life nevertheless continues for the others, and it ought not to become impoverished or meaningless because of his decision, but rather gain a new import and increased reasons for being affirmed.

Just as there is a total treasury of prayer, so, too, in particular, is there a treasury of the time of choice, a treasury of consent and of gleaming example. Every newly spoken consent, every example that is given in such a consent, belongs to the Church in an intimate way and is further dispensed by her. It is the Church's to administer. The Church keeps none of her treasures for herself. She no more locks up her spiritual provisions than she removes her monstrances and vestments in cathedrals from use. They are there in order to be seen, used and lived. No consent stands isolated. Each and every consent is related to a future one or an already spoken one, and to every other consent.

Every Yes that is spoken gives the Church's Yes to God more weight, more meaning and "gravitational pull" for those who still have to utter their Yes, or to those for whom it has in the meantime become difficult to have once uttered theirs. A new wave is added to the Church's circulatory system; the interchange becomes a livelier, more vibrant, more significant event. In this way, the apostolate of the one newly called has, above all, to do with his attitude or, what is more, with the attitude of the Church.

Each word of Scripture now appears new to the one called, and it exhibits a sense he had never discovered until now. Each word opens up and communicates a great deal. But, through the consent of the one called, Scripture acquires a new sense also for the Church. It is as if the spiritual nourishment had become tastier and had come closer to one's reach. The branches of the tree that is the Church and their contents participate in the newness and living quality of a fresh consent. There are many who grow fatigued in contemplation and reading of the Scriptures. Even if they do take up the Holy Scriptures, they no longer find much that is new or useful in them. But if they can once see the change brought about by the Scriptures and the Church in a soul called by God, this does not remain without effect on them.

IV

ESTRANGEMENT FROM SELF
THROUGH THE RULE

Christ was a man among other men, but he was one who allowed himself to be formed and guided by the Father and the Holy Spirit. He wanted to be the man that the Father had planned at the creation, a man who would not bear the name of Second Adam in vain. Through love and continual obedience he wanted to present to us the original image of man that the Father had conceived. He moved about freely, he did what the others did. He lived in his parents' house, learned a trade and exercised it. But whatever he did, he never deviated from that original image. And his word was the eternal Word of the Father, with a meaning given by the Father and accepted by the Son. This giving and accepting was an expression of the uninterrupted dialogue between Father and Son. He is the Father's Word, and this Word is meant for him. He *is* the Word and he lives in it. And when he speaks this Word he gives men the Word of Heaven, to their benefit. He shows them the Father's designs, but also his love, in which they may live just as sheltered as he. His Word is a heavenly and eternal shelter for men, and the Father wants to give it to them in the Son.

On earth, the Son lives the Father's mandate, and the

rule of its implementation is the Holy Spirit. The love, because of which the Son was to become man, was not a blind love. It knew what it was undertaking: the mandate to live on earth in the Holy Spirit and to let what was his own pass over into what is the Spirit's. Through the Holy Spirit the Son indicates the Father's divinity. Not for a moment does he depart from his mandate. And in this obedience to the Father through the rule of the Spirit, he brings the world back to God.

Everyone, therefore, who has chosen the way of discipleship can always look to the Son and ask himself what the Son would have done in his position. The answer is always the same: he would have done whatever corresponded to his "rule", which is to say the Holy Spirit. He would have chosen what the Father had chosen for him. And so the person who, choosing, is himself chosen, understands that he must do what the Son did. He understands that what is at stake is not fashioning for oneself a personality according to one's own invented laws; what is at stake is passing over into obedience, and this obedience is wide and strict enough to allow each one the space and to give each one the form that God has intended for him.

Up to the moment of choice and of the acceptance of obedience, there had been numerous rules to which the person felt bound—rules stemming from the parental home, from his career and education, from his plans and activities. He accepted all these rules freely, by recognizing their necessity, and he allowed himself to be formed by them from the outside and to be developed from within. Without thinking about it expressly, he must have realized the justification of this asceticism for his development and his work. He wore this ascesis like a garment, and it distinguished him from others by belonging to his work and, more deeply, to his very being. Many of these rules remained opaque and could easily be bypassed; others again were of the most pressing necessity. Some of them he had come to cherish; with others he was never on friendly terms. But all along he considered himself a free person. And, in fact, many of his decisions did depend on his discretion. Once the decision was made, however, he had to submit to the consequences, both the foreseen and the desired, and also those which remained unknown, unwished for and unmerited.

Now that he has chosen obedience as his rule in order to follow the Lord, he must give back that to which he had grown accustomed. He must give it back with freedom, because he has chosen something greater in its place, with a freedom that places itself on the scales along with everything else. He will no longer be able to contribute to the formation of his rule. From now on there will be a strict either/or. The rule belongs to the Holy Spirit. He must love it and accept it just as it is. He cannot ask it to be twisted for his sake, nor can he raise any objections and demand that superiors take into account he is used to this and that, or that he is this or that kind of person, so valuable, in fact, that order and rule should make an exception in his case, since they are so enriched by his presence. He must make himself as nothing; he must allow himself to be effaced until he has become a stranger to himself, so stripped that he cannot recognize his own nakedness and can hardly formulate the object of his desires. For he has chosen love; and indeed not a limited, nameable love, but God's absolute love; so one and so absolute that it passes over him without any apparent concern for him, without even noticing his existence. The edifice that he has been carefully erecting in the course of the years has begun to falter at the first blowing of the Spirit. Only when he can no longer recognize either himself or what he is, is he fully capable of recognizing God's answer and his will, capable of accepting his rule as the rule of the Holy Spirit. The desired destruction and effacement can be very painful. But in any event, it is salutary because, following it, God's work can take place without hindrance. Not only has the visible edifice collapsed with its advantages and disadvantages but, along with it, everything which was an obstacle has been basically overcome: conscious and unconscious factors, noticeable and secret, things one loves and things one hates. The person has become so distant from himself that every space in him has become free for the reception of law and of love. Whether the love of God manifests itself in a storm or in a barely perceptible whisper, it is always strong enough to blow away everything and make room for the new life. It is capable of completing the work of estrangement. The remains of the old edifice that lie scattered about offer a strange and perhaps laughable sight. What had seemed put together for a lifetime proved to be so transitory that nothing remains with recognizable shape.

Now, the person who encounters the love of God in the midst of his own wreckage and has had the period of estrangement from himself must pray for the grace of perseverance. Everything would have been in vain if already the next day he begins to weave himself a new garment out of his own nakedness or to build himself a new house with the ruins of who he was, again clinging to what was his own, again fashioning plans and behaving as if God's rule had at all costs to be subjected to his own laws. What is new must remain new and is not allowed to become old. The consent must retain its full resonance.

Since the rule is given in the Holy Spirit, it in some way has an absolute character, but insofar as it is administered by men, certain changes and adaptations are necessary. These, however, may not proceed from the person who has been submitted to the rule. The living quality of the rule is so great that, without surrendering its clarity, it is capable of being interpreted in many different ways. This is analogous to the manner in which the mystery of God's Trinity is at the same time univocal in its interior order and yet infinitely manifold in its aspects. In each article of faith one discovers new approaches to that mystery. The rule came to be with the help of the Holy Spirit. It possesses something of the fullness of eternal life, which always remains richer than every attempt to comprehend it with thought. Whoever subjects himself to the rule for the first time must seek its explanation from those experienced in keeping it for a long time. He can formulate questions, but in the answers he receives he must see the norm he must abide by, at least temporarily. And he must remain aware of the fact that what he has reigning over him is not a letter or a formula, but a Spirit, a life. He adheres to the Church and to God, not as he would to dead concepts, but to living realities. But the rule presents a stricter norm than does the Church; obedience in an order gives shape to everyday life much more precisely. This is not so only because particular acts are either prescribed or forbidden to him, but simply because of the fact that he stands under an obedience that is forming him almost without his being able to realize or confirm the process. Along with the others who are under the same rule, he swims in a communal stream, and he must let the current take its course without supervising it from the standpoint of his previous life, without making it dependent on present moods. He also knows very clearly that this is *God's* rule and that in his weakness he will never be able to keep it perfectly. It was fully kept only *once:* by the Son in the Father's Presence. But the Son is the Way, the Life and the Truth, and whoever faithfully follows him can trust that the Son will be for him, too, the gate that leads to the Father. To live in the rule means always to stand at this gate without ever leaving it behind. The love for men of the Son, and also of the Father and the Holy Spirit, flows forth unceasingly from this gate. It is the locus of living grace.

When Joan of Arc answers her judges that if she is not in grace she hopes to attain it, then she is indeed standing at this gate. It is a place where no further statements concerning one's "I" are possible, a place where only perseverance in love and discipleship remains. From the moment of consent and thereafter, every believer is in a position of following this example, without detours, straight to the Son. And all tasks imposed by the rule—those of self-perfection, of obedience, even of studies and of the liturgy—are tasks of love which even a whole lifetime cannot bring to conclusions. No one can say he has finished these tasks of love and that now he has room for something entirely different. He cannot say this because it is the rule which has imposed the task and because the liveliness of the task is rooted in the greater liveliness of the rule. The believer may not at any cost remove the task from this mother-soil in order to fashion a task formed and designed by him alone. He should, on the contrary, preserve a living bond between task and rule, and always see it and accept it anew from that standpoint. If this living quality is the norm of his activity, the believer's exile from himself will be guaranteed, and this norm will engage him in a process that will make him resemble the Son in his mission ever more exactly.

The wording of the rule is definitive, and it resounds down from such a height that not only is more said to the believer than he will ever be able to understand, but things that are urgent are exacted of him in the present in such ample supply that this alone should suffice to guarantee the liveliness of the rule. The words of the rule are words of the Spirit, analogous to the way the Son remains the Father's Word. One can no more adapt the wording of the rule to one's personal needs than one can provide a new meaning to the Son's words for one's own private use. By accepting the efficacious and fruitful words of the rule in his heart, the believer should learn to bear fruit in a Christian sense, and he will thereby find himself exiled from what he had hitherto been, like a woman who, having conceived, is transformed by the fruit growing within her and becomes estranged from herself. The child gains ascendance in her and the mother becomes a function. In the same way the believer becomes a function of the Word. In Mary, both things coincide: the Child *is* the Word. At the moment of surrendering herself, she knows approximately what is involved: estrangement from self in love. This love grows in her in order to rule her and form her in an ever more exhaustive manner.

V

POVERTY

Among the basic concepts of a normal middle class life we find that of every sort of "construction". A young person acquires knowledge and makes it his own in order to be able to turn it into something useful later on. And even if the youth did not himself come to this idea unaided, his environment is quite certain to make him stumble upon it. Like knowledge, so too every other kind of intellectual and material enrichment, every type of financial or intellectual "capital" is integrated into the total plan of the "construction" of his life. His future life is full of expectations from him: from what he is and even more from what he has. He hears prosperity being praised in every possible key. And if he studies the catalog of securities offered he will realize that one can insure himself in every possible direction: against sickness and accidents, against property damage and theft and disability, and all of these insurances are intended to ward off but one thing, poverty. Even the implementation of his "knowledge" will help him to establish his well-being more solidly and to find a better position.

But if he once chooses the way of Christ's discipleship, he must suddenly give up this whole point of view. He renounces the material, and even the intellectual no longer is guaranteed to be used. One would urgently have to warn him before entering an order against giving too much thought to the question of how much guarantee he has that his talents will be profitably used in his new life. God wants him for himself. Neither his mind, however, nor his body, nor his health, nor his education or experiences, henceforth have an absolute value. God wants only him, and he wants him so much that he renounces everything else that may still be connected with him. He wants him, not accompanied by his worldly securities, but naked. A new life is beginning, and God himself will provide it with what he judges to be good. Perhaps he will select this or that from his previous state and entrust it to him, but then again, maybe not. This is the way of poverty, of a poverty that *wants* to be poor and that strips itself, the way of a nakedness and a particular solitude that belong to poverty. And all these things to which a person until now thought to have a natural claim—his clothes, his bed—all of it is part of what is given him as a gift, of what he must ask and be thankful for. He no longer has to determine the organization of these things, nor their quality or arrangement. He should, rather, be amazed that someone still feeds him, thinks of his need for rest and even provides him with further education.

All of this, after all, is a gift coming to him from God's grace without his having a claim to it. Through the gesture of self-stripping he remains a strict disciple of the Lord. This is a Christian gesture, because it is a gesture of Christ, a divine gesture. The Son hung naked on the Cross. Naked did he come into the world. He lived in poverty and gave everything back to the Father, even his spirit. In the life of the one called there is no section in which at least something of this law does not become manifest. It may be that in certain respects he now seems to be better off than in his previous life. But the opposite is also possible. Whatever the case may be, he possesses nothing but rather has everything on loan. And the end-purpose of what he has been given is no longer his own, but God's. The more perfect the poverty, the more perfect will the discipleship be. The standard, however, is not external deprivation to extremes of hunger and misery, but spiritual attitude. Only where poverty is perfected does it become evident how great God's grace is, and how it brings a person to God. He now relies on the Father, like the birds of heaven and the flowers of the field that are clothed by him. He relies on the Father even more than these others, whom God preserves through natural laws, since the poor man lives in direct dependence on God. He does it without many questions and cares. Preoccupations and assurances and thinking back to what has been are all attacks on poverty.

It can be that the act of letting go succeeds with one stroke; everything is left behind and nothing is pined after. But it can also be that things enjoyed such a legitimacy in the mind of their owner that he can adopt the new standpoint only with the greatest effort. Poverty makes his whole inner world falter and even dashes it to pieces. The questions could possibly arise: "To what extent was all of this justified as long as I live in the world? Was it right for me to study, to earn money, to have savings and to take more in order to increase my fortune? Or, was this manner of living already in itself false? And was it perhaps so firmly buttressed in order that this other way of life—which is now mine—might appear all the more unbearable and precarious? Did reason hold such powerful sway in my everyday life so that the folly of the Cross might appear all the more crass?"

There are many things about this renunciation that are difficult to achieve. Old-standing habits, for instance, that had been adopted in order to secure something about one's life—intellectual work, and better concentration: even these are rejected along with everything else; not only questioned, but simply given up. In the new life the same questions can arise as in the old: "Wouldn't it be reasonable to keep, ask for and defend those things which I by right had and which fostered my capacity to achieve?" Here again the one called must renew his contemplation of the Son. The Son laid down no conditions for the Father. He accepted human life just as the Father offered it to him. He lived each day as the Father presented it to him. He turned every encounter and every conversation into God's affair, the affair of the Father, giving it over to him as the most natural thing to do and holding nothing back for himself. Since perfect renunciation and poverty are achieved only by the Son, the one called will soon realize the many possibilities poverty offers for discipleship. Poverty, indeed, becomes a wealth which he would no longer do without for anything in the world. Poverty becomes the guarantee that he will never be hampered on his way to the Son, a guarantee that wherever he perceives a hint of the Son, or a tremor of grace attracts him, he will not be held back by the proportions of his own possessions, will not stumble on what is lifeless when he is seeking life, will not have to take the side of the deniers when he knows what ought to be affirmed. Everyone, moreover, who with Saint Francis consecrates himself to poverty because he sees in her a way of unhindered discipleship, will introduce into the existence of men seeking for God new openings, new forms of ascent and of self-surrender. Even as he points the way to renunciation and seems thereby to be depriving them of something, the one called is, in fact, giving them a gift. This gift is faith, the nearness and liveliness of the Word.

An unbeliever who considers his life has to see that he began in a state of nakedness and that he will end up between the walls of a coffin. He will again lose everything he has. But he will, perhaps, not realize how much of his time, his talents and his abilities are eaten up by possessions, how many thoughts he squanders on them, how many good and important things are lost to possessions—to say nothing of the abundance of God's presence. The one called, on the contrary, thanks God that he has been allowed to give everything away. He has experienced the fact that, in giving, one is confronted by the gift of God and that, in his act of giving, man is outdone by God's gift to him. The movement of giving away that he makes is continued in the receiving of what God holds out to him.

The rule is the wealth of the order. The rule is what it possesses and what gives it character, what distinguishes it from other orders and makes it recognizable. As something given to the founder by the Holy Spirit in hours of grace—an agreement arrived at in the founder's dialogue with God—the rule is not the product of an overheated fantasy or of spiritual presumption, but a fruit of contemplation. It is the distinguishing mark proper to the order, which is given to it anew with each novice in untouchable integrity. It is a sign of present life, of the Holy Spirit's continued assistance, of the fact that the founder continues to live in the spirit. The hour of grace at the foundation still has its validity today. In the Church, it is a small analogy to the way in which God's word remains living and present to Sacred Scripture. The reality of discipleship, God's participation in the life of his people, everything he offers them is a present wealth. But whoever says "wealth" in a Christian sense knows also the power of poverty. A lukewarm compromise is excluded. Those called must be poor in all things in order to be rich in the rule. They renounce worldly things in order to acquire that which is spiritual and divine. Pole and counterpole stand against each other, and only through this polarity can be gained what can only be described as life in God. Only in this way does life remain a living and flowing thing. This movement can express itself as either contemplation or active life. Action goes to the poor of this world—"poor" in whatever sense—in order to bring them God's wealth. Contemplation goes back to the days of the founder, when heaven stood open and the Spirit descended, and even more deeply it goes back to the continual presence of the Spirit in the Church, in order to proclaim the liveliness of this presence in all the Church's organs: in Scripture, in the orders, in the forms of discipleship.

The rule prescribes the form poverty will assume in particular instances. This expression, too, is a sign of its wealth. Everyone comes with a definite opinion concerning poverty and wealth. He comes as one who, being chosen, is perhaps more occupied with the life that awaits him than with the choice itself. Up to a certain point he must leave the future to God, and yet he does not want to enter that future in total darkness. He already knows people who live under the rule, and the words of the rule have somehow left their mark on him already in the time before his entrance. But he was still an outsider; he had his own ideas about world, vocation and entrance into the religious life and he let the words of the rule have their effect upon him just as he was. Once he has entered, however, and once the rule has become the exclusive norm of his life, the focal point of the rule must assume a central position in his life. His opinions are suddenly deprived of their rights; he must put them off like the rest of his possessions, and allow himself to be deeply affected by the substance of the rule. The rule itself now acquires a new effectiveness; it exhibits a new aura of variety, or perhaps also the dullness of monotony; but in any event, it behaves in a way undesired by him, a way he *must* now desire, since God wills it.

As one grows older the infirmities of age and the increasing burden of daily life remind many a person of the Lord's word to Peter: "You will be led where you do not want to go." He wanted to remain a healthy, energetic, self-reliant man, and now he is led to the Cross. Through the acceptance of the rule something similar happens, at the same time a premature aging and being led where one does not want to go. But this is precisely the prerequisite for a new youth, one that no longer follows biological laws, but which blossoms abruptly and unexpectedly and, because of its very suddenness, evades every attempt at investigation. The rule has its own law. It sifts, selects, admits and rejects: the system erected by one's own ideas is thoroughly demolished. Its place is taken by the living and unsurveyable system of the Holy Spirit. Whether this is a hard thing or not is indifferent. If only the life of the one called has truly been surrendered, then it is caught up in the living quality of the rule.

Sacred Scripture becomes a more pressing reality for the one who has been formed by the liveliness of the rule, and he becomes much more conscious of the Lord's presence in the Eucharist. From God's nearness and efficacy there flows a transforming energy. It is as if things should now be revalued, as if they should all be deleted and created anew, as if a spring had suddenly burst forth where there had been nothing but barren, dried-up earth. With every Christian miracle there is experienced something similar to what keeps the rule a living thing: the impossible becomes possible, what is dead comes to life, what is sickly is shot through with new forces, a No becomes a Yes and many a Yes receives the power of changing into a No. I speak of something like an effervescence, a becoming, a birth and much new fertility. Possibilities now awaken that had been ignored or let lie fallow and slumbering. These are the ways of a living faith, in a manifoldness whose inner structure fully escapes the one affected by it. There is no way he could know that just because the Spirit has come to life in him through the rule, astounding things are happening in far-off lands, or perhaps in his immediate proximity: what has wilted begins to bloom again, an old word gains new power, a petrified kind of Christianity transforms itself into a ready willingness and self-surrender.

One's own ideas had earlier proved to be good in a thousand ways. Their correctness could be backed by numbers and personal experiences. They had had a conquering power which had been exercised, at first cautiously, then with more certitude and self-confidence, in occupying ever-new territories. Everything was made into a horizon to be quantified and subjected to one's reason. Under the rule everything is different. Its liveliness derives ultimately, not from an ordering reason, but from poverty in the face of the Spirit. All situations of existence in which the one called is involved are filled with the breath of the living Spirit and shaped by him. At times one can almost touch him with one's hands. At other times he is hardly perceptible, present only to faith. But the Spirit is always there.

Until this point the person had always given a personal slant to his experiences. Even his intellectual achievements had been "touched up" subjectively with the greatest care. His opinions and world view had been daintily nursed and fostered. In the new life all of this stops. He must stand so naked and cleared of accoutrements that there will be space for the rule and for the wealth that comes solely from it. Things are now defined anew, words and concepts shift their nuances, no longer in a personal sense but from the viewpoint of the Spirit. The person has become a vessel and only his poverty is left. A wind has blown away all that was his, and he can no longer say in a worldly sense: "*my* opinions, *my* studies, *my* faith". Whatever is there to be had is the property of the triune God.

VI

OBEDIENCE

To be a child of God means to be obedient, to draw on an obedience that has its source in the obedience of the Son himself, in order to live by it. Obedience is not an attitude with respect to God that may be interpreted by a person in any way he wishes. God's Son became obedient unto death, and this neither from passivity nor from resignation and a hollow sense of *laissez-faire*, but from love. It is love that lets things happen, that puts up with and even accepts passively those things it must. Love gives "attitudes" their true significance, even those attitudes opposed to itself.

The Lord is obedient in a double sense. First of all, he is obedient to the Father and to his task. At no moment does he take his mission into his hands as belonging solely to him, in order to turn it into a possession and shape it as seems most fit to him. His mission remains in the hands of the Father, and from the Father's will he deciphers what the Father intends for him, and, simply, what the Father desires. And, while always looking in this way in the Father's direction, he remains in obedience. As a man, however, he also remains obedient with regard to his fellow men. Mary and Joseph have in him an obedient son who learns human ways from them as any person in the world and who is pliant to their judgment. Indeed, he does this in such a way that he never measures the distance between his human parents and his Father in heaven so as to discover a discrepancy somewhere in their views and commands and so create for himself a "conflict of duties". He knows that his parents are themselves bound to the triune God. He knows that they themselves have accepted their tasks in obedience and that a part of their task consists of instilling in him a humanly understood obedience. By obeying them he fulfills Mary's and Joseph's own obedience, and because of this obedience, or rather *along with it,* he fulfills his eternal obedience to the Father. He creates a unity with every form of obedience that he encounters, with every form of obedience that comes into contact with his own responsibility and that is willingly accepted.

This unity in obedience also determines his life. There exists an uninterrupted continuity between his obedience as a small child and his obedience on the Cross. It is the task of the small child to follow up on what has been told him according to his child's understanding. The words of his Mother and his foster-father themselves move in a medium of obedience and asceticism. They do not speak for the sake of speaking; their words have a sense of faith and of fulfillment based on their own obedience. They do not "lecture" at the child. He does not have to listen to an abstract "quintessence" of divine dogma and he has no need to crawl in and out of the steep lattice-work of theological concepts. This child is reared in the freedom of love. He perceives love's words and takes them to himself.

Everyone who believes, through his obedience to the
Word, receives a mandate from the Word to cultivate
dialogue in a Christian manner. Even during the times
of recreation there is no such thing as "being free" of
the Word. There are no "holidays" from the Word, no
permission to take time out to become inebriated with
the music of one's own words or to engage in a conversation just for the sake of talking. Responsibility to the
Word knows no time-out, but neither does it constitute
the contrary of human play, cheerfulness and recreation.
When the Child Jesus plays with his Mother, he does
not play out of a sense of duty, but for sheer pleasure,
and the same holds for the Mother. And yet, in this play
the Word remains alive, it remains an ascetical attitude,
faith itself. Work and recreation proceed from the same
spirit. A word spoken during play remains as alive in
the Son as any other word. When later as a man he
proclaims the Father's teachings, he will in no way have
to distance his Word from the tone of his words as a
child. The Word is earnest, significant, disciplined, obedient and nevertheless it is chosen in freedom and is an
enrichment for everyone who hears it. It fructifies the
work in the Lord's vineyard, and this fruitfulness
nowhere excludes play, celebration and recreation.

Obedience becomes more immediately and tangibly
manifest in the twelve-year-old as he goes about the
affairs of his Father in his Father's house. His obedience
is not at first seconded by his parents' understanding. In
anguish they search for the obedient and considerate
child they had always known. But in the meantime, the

sense of a more far-reaching and more binding obedience has become disclosed to him, and the sense of their own obedience has thereby entered a new phase. When the angel visited Mary, much that had been latent in her—unused and unformulated—suddenly awakened and filled with life. The situation of the choice—God calls and she must answer—bestows a new dimension on her obedience. As always with one who obeys, she must utter her consent; but this consent is so stringently and so abruptly submerged in the unknown and present mystery of God's action that a new sphere of her obedience is thereby revealed. She must release her consent, putting it freely at God's disposal, in order that it may there blossom. It is taken up by God and, indeed, in an invisible manner.

With each day of her child's life, up to the very days of the Cross, the Resurrection, and the Ascension, she will experience her own obedience as a continually living thing, and she will discover that it contains more far-reaching consequences and more energetic and inexhaustible life than she had suspected. She experiences this in the things that occur to the Son, and perhaps the first experience of this kind is the anguished search for the lost child. A gap, a rift has opened up. The parents search for the Son, while the Son has found the Father in a new way and is realizing a part of his mission that had hitherto remained in the dark. It could be that he had seen the new exigencies approach day by day. Would he not some day have to stay in the Temple to interpret the Scriptures before the doctors of the Law and to reveal the Father's mysteries? But it could also be that the Father's call to do this occurred very suddenly. Whatever the case may be, he could not spare his parents the search for him. Even in the obedience of the most obedient, gaps, holes, missing links come to light for which God alone is responsible. Those who obey must, for this reason, lay their obedience bare in order that God might fill up the empty spaces. They must render their obedience without strings attached, so that it will no longer be their possession, fully transparent in every detail. The transparency lies in God. And when the human eye is no longer capable of figuring things out, the obeyer knows that God sees everything and administers obedience precisely as *his* possession. In its every phase, obedience is a gift to God, a surrender, but in ever-increasing intensity it becomes acceptance by God. The express obedience of the vows has its model in the Yes of the Lord's Mother as it is accepted by God. And in the Son's Yes to the Father it has a model even more deeply rooted in God. The Son's consent is only imperfectly fulfilled in the consent of the person who dares to say Yes; but it is fulfilled with utmost perfection in God as he receives and accepts it.

St. Paul's short formulation "made obedient unto the Cross", distills the whole of the Lord's way. On this road there is no pausing, no thinking things over: obedience leads straight to death, to the death that is already discerned in the Lord's mission. This is no symbolic death, to be understood in a purely spiritual sense, but a very hard reality. Looking back from the Cross we can follow the whole path. The observer can distinguish different segments and gradations in that path, but the one walking upon it cannot. He accepts Cross, Resurrection, and Ascension out of the same obedience with which he had received his Mother's words as a child. His obedience does not crumble to pieces with time and it cannot be grasped in fragments. His obedience is like an iron of one cast, an obedience out of love, and love that is really love knows no boundaries or reservations.

Whoever assents to obedience in this way utters an indivisible Yes. The energy of this consent lies in the Spirit. The Spirit who overshadows the Mother not only makes the obedient, divine Son come into being in her; it encounters her at the same time as mother, woman and believer, and makes her consent attain to a perfect fullness. In the Mother we cannot separate the spiritual from the bodily event. There occurs a passage from the spiritual to the bodily—the Child himself! In her there takes place a unified spiritual-bodily event that transcends the natural capabilities both of her spirit and of her body. An earthly standard cannot be applied to any of this, since the Spirit himself holds the standard in his hands. He meets that standard and he alone knows it. This standard has its visible effects both in the Mother's spirit and in her body, but this visibility itself bears the signs of its origin in the Spirit. It is a standard that disappears into God's invisible standard. Something similar occurs in every instance of Christian obedience. Something is promised that escapes human

standards and which can be neither judged nor measured by reason and reflection. Just as a prayer is accepted
by God and then exercises its effects in the most unexpected and unsuspected places, so too does obedience
have its effects purely according to God's judgment.
God alone gives the power, but the Spirit remains in
the act of overshadowing and of accepting what is
brought about. The Spirit accompanies every moment
of the Son's life as a Spirit of obedience. It is he who has
in his hands the standard of the Cross, a standard surpassing human thought. And when the dying Son gives
his Spirit back to the Father, he does something that
every obedient person can do after him: gives back to
the Father his obedience itself, which the Spirit has
borne, in order that the Father might foster it in himself,
making it fruitful.

At the moment when he gives his Spirit back, the
Son attains the fullness of his weakness. In his life as a
man, in his mission and in his suffering he has used up
all the forces the Father had entrusted to him. But the
Son cannot, on that account, discontinue his obedience.
Weakness and death merely keep him from continuing
to exercise an active kind of obedience, and in order to
preserve it whole and total the Son hands it over to the
Father. It is somewhat like a mother who is carrying her
child in her arms and who, on stumbling and feeling
she is about to fall, instinctively first looks to the safety
of the child. The giving back of the spirit guarantees
that Christ's obedience will remain intact. Whoever is
vowed to obedience and later on cannot carry it out or

find his way in it, whoever is vowed to obedience and then suffers under it, believing he is no longer able to bear it, will in every case have to give his spirit back to the Father along with the Cross with which he has been burdened, in order that the Father will himself administer the person's obedience and preserve it from being shattered.

It would be a mistake, however, to want to find obedience only at the Cross. Whoever wishes to be obedient must be so as much on the good days as on the difficult ones, and he must not be troubled if obeying comes easily to him. Even though the Son knew exactly the kind of Cross that awaited him, we cannot say that he let its shadow cast a gloom over every moment of his life. There was his childhood, the thirty years of the hidden life, the feasts and other joyful events of the public life, each of them with the appropriate atmosphere even though they were all a part of the way of the Cross. The fruit of Christ's suffering for us is so great that to many an obeyer it is granted to live in the certainty of Christ's having suffered for us, and he is not allowed to yearn for the Cross out of his own impulse and against the will of God. God distributes as he will, and, precisely because he obeys, the obeyer must not meddle with what God proposes to do with the Cross. This does not mean that we are spared asceticism. We remain open for every grace of the Lord's suffering. The fact that we ourselves do not preside over what will be our share is an expression of our self-surrender.

If obedience effects a unity between the obeying

person and God, who presides over obedience, then the
superior, who in the eyes of the Church holds the office
of leading others, must not become an obstacle or a
limiting intervention in this unity. He must not blur the
visibility between the obeyer and God, but must become
transparent to God. He will, of course, have his own
character, personality and spiritual orientation, but,
insofar as he holds that office, he possesses all of this,
not to do with as he wishes, but in a surrender that
makes him too, for his part, amenable to being transformed. His transparency results from a situation where
those entrusted to him and his own obedience together
collaborate with the action of God.

In the Gospel, the Lord is presented to us as stemming from a mighty genealogical tree that contains the
most varied figures and characters, all of them marked
with their own particularity. The Lord comes from his
own branch, with a history of its own, and his humanity bears the stamp of these factors. This "stamp" in no
way restricts his obedience. The stamp belongs to a
personality which, in turn, is not restricted by its perfect obedience. As obedient Son of the Father, Christ
does not become impersonal, since even in being obedient he is both God and Person, and together with the
Father he effects the procession of the Holy Spirit. Nor
does the pliancy of his human nature before his divine
Person make that nature impersonal. Rather does his
humanity enhance its freshness and uniqueness by that
submission, even as it is determined by his ancestors, his
birth from Mary the Virgin, the education Joseph gave

him, and by growing up in a certain environment and culture. Jesus is not "anyone", nor is he "everyone": he is himself. And precisely as such a particular person is he the way to the Father. His particular traits become prominent exactly to the degree called for by his obedience and by his function of being the way to the Father. What he is in his human uniqueness is not bracketed when he says of himself that he is the Way, the Truth and the Life. His uniqueness in no way blurs his being transparent to God. And from us he demands an obedience that is formed from the very substance of his own obedience to the Father.

A child obeys his mother simply because she is the mother, with her superior knowledge of things. The child feels the necessity of obeying. As the child grows, something of this necessity does, indeed, remain; but his obedience becomes more personal and refined, and it now also involves wishes and intentions that the mother has never stated explicitly. An understanding awakens in the child for a spiritual line of action which he now tries to abide by. He can now acquire a bad conscience for actions that had not been expressly forbidden.

Something similar occurs with the obedience of the one called. There is, of course, the external breaking of the rule. But, at the same time, there is always an unformulated element that is voluntarily assumed in order to be obedient to the Spirit in the spirit, obedient to a Spirit that has never become an explicit letter. And there is also an obedience that is more than obedience, a voluntary state that rounds off necessity and gives it a totally new appearance, and which also shapes all previous willingness anew. This mystery may already be discovered in the Lord's words during his Passion: "Not my will, but yours be done." In spite of the fundamental identity of the Father's and the Son's will, the congruence of the two is here sought again and, indeed, found. It is not as if, as a man, the Son had ever lost this unity. But it is maintained, not in mere passivity, rather in a lively exchange of giving and receiving. Something similar should always be the case with an adult's obedience; there should ever be at work a renewed sense for what is willed and desired at the present moment, so as to launch upon it in a living manner. The obeyer should not always be looking around for analogies in the history of his order, or in the proximate or distant climate of the order, so as to ascertain in juridical fashion what he is bound or not bound to. His obedience should be, rather, spontaneous, willing surrender, a listening to what is expected of him and an unreflecting, joyful acceptance of it.

When we think of the Person of the Son, and of the might of his mission, and of the power of the love with which he envelops the Father, we must time and again marvel at the fact that he wishes to be nothing other than the Gate. He humbles and annihilates himself to such an extent that what constantly becomes visible is the unimpeded view of the Father, and he becomes the embodiment of all truth belonging to the Father. To be sure, it is his obedience that expropriates him in this way; but he is not repressed as person, until he becomes something like a hollow space or a thoroughfare. Rather does he do all of this out of a willing love, so that love comes to occupy every space in him and, through him, attains its every effect. Through love he reveals the Father. In this manner, the one called, having chosen the way of the Son's obedience, can make himself an instrument of pure love, a love that shines forth because the obeyer steps into the background, a love that makes him into a living pointer of the Way.

VII

VIRGINITY

"How is this possible, since I do not know any man?", asks Mary of the angel. Precisely as a virgin is she supposed to bear the Son. The greatest nearness possible between two human beings—the mother's bearing of her child—is granted to Mary by reason of her virginity. Everything else recedes for the time being, to return only later. As a virgin she becomes the Mother of the Lord, both Bride and Church. As a virgin will she go through the different natural and supernatural phases and stages of a woman's life. She will conceive, bear the Son and rear him and then, unnoticed, she will grow into her role as Bride of Christ and thus be transformed into the very beginning of his Church. Everything is included in her first Yes, because this Yes was an unconditional one. And if it could be unconditional, it was because the Lord had redeemed her in advance, having chosen her from all eternity and found her to be worthy.

Everything, however, that is accomplished in her or is done by her occurs for the sake of the future Church. It occurs likewise for the sake of the Son who comes to the world through her and who becomes the Founder and Bridegroom of the Church. Accordingly, nothing in her life is left up to chance, everything about her is of the deepest significance for the Lord and for the Church. This significance is to be found where the mysteries of bodily-spiritual fruitfulness have their home, where the relationship of perfect closeness is made possible and union with the God who became man is prepared and achieved.

In her *fiat,* Mary is all surrender and acquiescence. Following from this attitude, her body, too, is surrendered in a new way. Until now it had remained in a kind of expectation and indifference, not to be distinguished from the expectation of any girl who remains a virgin. Such indifference of expectation is suddenly taken up into the choice by the words of the angel. Mary will remain a virgin, but at the same time, in a way unknown to anyone either before or after her, she will be bound to the God who becomes man. The road of her solitude is indicated by the Lord himself, in keeping with her consent, a consent that is so unique and so perfect that she will never enter into conflict with it. Her body and the totality of her life on earth place themselves at the disposal of that consent. She wastes no time asking, "What are the things you will demand? How will you make it possible?" She only mentions briefly the fact of her virginity in order that we might realize her renunciation and see it as the point of departure of the perfect following of Christ. In the future, everything she does as the Lord's companion occurs within the context of her virginity, a condition that poses no further questions for her. That is the way it is and it will never change.

Already, starting at the Cross, she becomes the matrix of all that is to come and the very source of the Church. For that reason she gives her virginity to the Church as her most intimate dowry. Her virginity is so fruitful that it will suffice for all who will later utter their consent. Each person called tries to speak the word of virginity in imitation of her. In her, each person sees his own virginity already fully developed, and he understands that his own questionableness, limitations and unreadiness find their solution in her. The simplicity and purity of her being is both intended for each person and decisive of his discipleship.

Problems are solved by her consent. But this does not mean that, as the question of virginity is raised for many a person, he will not have to think seriously of his past, his temptations and his whole attitude with regard to the problem. He must admit his weaknesses to himself, and perhaps will regret the fact that he has perceived God's request only today, since he has to give God an answer burdened by such a "past". He must, nevertheless, realize that the power for a total consent lies in the grace of the divine query. It is an overflowing power that does not merely — like a mountain torrent — roar away over all particular temptations, trains of thought and hesitations; this power, rather, resolves each thing interiorly. In God's great question and answer, the one called receives also the solution of his small questions. God's voice contains in itself the voice of the person who has assented to him, basing himself on Mary's Yes. The sinner's every hesitation has been overcome in advance by the unflinching Yes of her who is without sin.

Virginity's share in asceticism consists above all in an entering upon the road of the Lord's Mother, of her simplicity and blind trust. Virginity must become as blind as obedience does when demanded by God. In Mary, virginity is an act of abiding blindness, which is to say an act of perfect trust, of perfect handing over of self, indeed of *already* having handed oneself over, and this in such a thorough-going manner that the Mother learns her answer itself from the angel. When she goes to Elizabeth, moreover, her virginal nearness and the mystery of the fruit within her awaken her cousin's child to a new life of exultation: virginity has always had something to impart, even to those who, not living in it, still expect and receive from it a new fertility. Virginity becomes a universal gift of God to the Church, fruitful for everyone and deriving from its origin in the Mother in whom it was realized with no questions asked, and it is so rich in variations and modalities that its energy never dwindles. Out of her own trusting surrender, the Mother gives away what is hers and what, nevertheless, cannot be separated from what belongs to the Son. We here encounter the mystery of a fusion of her renunciation with the Son's own wealth, of her giving with the Son's taking, of her expectation with its fulfillment by the Son. And this fulfillment is rich enough always to fulfill anew, to fulfill even that which is *a priori* incompatible with virginity, but which nevertheless—although not equally oriented—belongs to the Church, along with virginity, in the manner of a completing and complementary fecundity. The Church does not turn anyone away. Even when fruitfulness is already at hand, as in Elizabeth's case, she puts the wealth of her virginity at everyone's disposal, in order to show its efficaciousness even there. Genuine virginity is always rich in its ability to *show*. It never implies narrowness, nor does it cast a grey tint over a person's everyday life or make him lonely. Virginity, rather, connotes participation in each mystery of the adult person and in the particular form of his relationship to God and to the Church, and it bestows on him a new state of being and energy. Virginity is so wholly derived from the power of the consent that this power continues to nourish it unceasingly. It is not misfits who submit to the asceticism of virginity, but renouncers who, through their renunciation, increase what others possess. It takes strong persons to give so much that they do not even look back after setting their hand to the plow. The purity and unencumberedness that characterize virginity point the way to love and understanding. No one can pray the simplest *Ave* or entertain the slightest thought concerning the Church without being influenced by the power of the virginal, whatever form it takes. Whoever remembers the Lord's Mother must think of her mysteries. What is most mysterious about her is the simplicity of a child of God. By her consent, she is transferred back to the unproblematic age of a child, not as if she had hitherto thought in a complicated manner which must now be simplified, but in the sense that everything in her which could have hardened into a question, leading to intricate conclusions and fostering moments of hesitating reflection—everything is now dissolved and evened out in a *childlike* manner, in the Theresian sense of the term. The "I choose all" of Thérèse of Lisieux implies nothing other than the unconditional nature of the consent and a person's perseverance in it.

The Church's virginity has its roots in Mary, the Mother of the Lord, whose attitude is preserved and continued by the Church as Mother of the Faithful. Such virginity is never an attitude of escape, evasion or fear, but of trust and surrender to God, a losing and giving away of oneself, body and soul, out of which God may let come whatever pleases him. It is something perfectly unconditional which in Mary perdures without a shadow of reservation. The angel encounters Joseph's bride; but her readiness is so great that she allows the angel to open up what, to her, seemed already closed and decided, even the fact of her inability to conceive, which for her was something established. It is actually not *her* problem, and, since it somehow arises for her nevertheless, it finds in God himself the answer that God had prepared in advance. Because Mary in advance allows the human to be taken up by the divine, an unheard-of expansion takes place in her. And the angel receives her consent like an echo whose power comes back to her again from heaven, inundating her, and it allows her to follow paths that will make, out of the Lord's bodily Mother, the spiritual Bride and birth-giving Church of the Apocalypse.

The person attempting to live as a disciple, however, will not find it so easy to distance himself from what he has become at an earthly level. Even when he wants to surrender himself to God, he still retains an old "I" that occupies him considerably. He would often like to take his consent back. He has often said "yes" with a kind of momentary trust, without considering that faith consists of more than only trust. And God tests him. Or the believer has not, perhaps, considered that God makes certain demands in the face of which a person can do nothing other than bear and patiently endure. Or one has traced one's own road in advance, letting the desires and impulses of the body run their course, and allowing them a room for play that suddenly expands and becomes so broad that regret immediately sets in. Or, on the contrary, this room for play proves to be so narrow that there is suddenly no escape in sight. The believer is now of the opinion he overestimated his forces, or that he engaged forces that were not even his. He hears of biological laws and is duly impressed. He remembers the words of Genesis: "Increase and multiply!" He thinks of these words as being a duty and an obligation for him. Diametrically opposed is the Lord's word to him that demands discipleship in an inexorable way. Now he is supposed to give up his most justified desires. Perhaps he will find a certain consolation in the figure of the Church, in the surrender of God's Mother to her Son, in the promises that have been fulfilled. But this can be quite an abstract sort of consolation, thought up for others, as it were. For him it seems to be insufficient. In good faith, to be sure, he has ventured into a dimension of renunciation to which he is not equal.

This is how the temptations appear that many another person before him has experienced. What if Paul *did* speak about the struggle of the saints? He himself is no Paul, and certainly no saint! To him it somehow seems presumptuous always to be reaching out for what is totally holy—the sacraments, for example—for what belongs to the divine dimension in the narrowest sense. Then, too, he has a need for feeling sheltered, a need for a finite sphere of influence: a home where his reason could come to bear. But his reason does not speak as does the Gospel. And yet, if only he has once penetrated to the renunciation's most interior fruitfulness, even to the "maternity" to be found in the Church's virginal being, then he will surely feel as one does after earnest prayer—filled with new forces and a confidence that open up a wide space before him. He will and must go on; he *shall* go on, since precisely *this* grace is offered him and it will not be he that will struggle and win, but the grace that is in him. For his part, he has struggled *against* grace for so long that he has the appearance of one defeated by grace. And yet, this victory of the Lord imparts to him a new knowledge concerning the body. He must now experience the collapse of his strongest arguments and the demolition of what he had erected around himself as a protection. Through this defeat he becomes a real believer, one whom the Lord has built up and the Church has formed; he becomes an image that will find its final perfection in eternal life. He remains a struggler. But God is the victor, and the person's future rests solely on this victory, as does the future of many others who are entrusted to him precisely on account of his renunciation, just as Christ and the Church had been entrusted to Mary the Virgin. Christ had been entrusted to her as the one Son, both God and Man, and the Church not merely as a supernatural institution, but along with all her carnal members, in such a way that no earthly maternity can be compared to the breadth and concreteness of Mary's motherhood.

The Lord's apostles and disciples all show very different faces and sorts of life. But they all walk on the one road—Christ. Between him and those who are his there is not only distance—as great as the distance between God and man—but also that which infinitely binds and equates, a unity and a similarity that the Lord himself has created and bestowed on his own so as to make their seemingly so different roads lead to the one Road. As they turn their glances toward him, their faces begin to resemble one another with a mysterious similarity. This is the Communion of Saints: the Church. In her we find remarkable saints who, nevertheless, are all Saints of the Church, living from the holiness of the triune God, of the Lord, and of his Mother. When someone utters his consent to the Son, thus entering his discipleship, and speaks the vow of virginity on whose power he intends to live, he does not perhaps know how mysterious and hidden is the power of such an act. There is in it a meeting of promise and fulfillment that for the one that carries it out can only be called a *new beginning*. No longer is it—as in the transition from the Old to the New Testament—a promise that passes over into fulfillment; it is, rather, the fulfillment in the Son and in the Mother that allows the promise to become a living thing for the new person making the vow. The chaste person lives in a promise that has already been permanently fulfilled outside of himself, a promise that envelops him with strength and life. The new life is the new fruitfulness in which he participates as a virgin. This is a fruitfulness that is freely available in the Church and which surrounds both the least of all and the mightiest, a fruitfulness that may be discerned here and there, but which has its source and origin in those vowed to virginity. The dynamism of prayer can be imagined as a line going from the one praying to God, and from God to that spot in the world where God wills to engage the effects of the prayer. With virginity, however, it is as if a fruitfulness shone forth from Christ and the Church in an incipient and evolving state, a fruitfulness on the verge of realization which, in order to blossom fully, needs the containing soil of a vow. The Church has countless children, some of whom attain to genuine sanctity and others who end up as pitiable sinners. It is the Church which alone disposes of God's sanctifying grace, giving meaning and force to every life, and it is from the Church alone that the vows receive their justification. Grace given through the Church bestows strength where there had been only weakness and misery. The virginal person, too, lives in a kind of weakness, since he has renounced his own strength. He remains in expectation because he does not himself strive to bring about the fulfillment, and he perseveres in readiness because he does not himself wish to determine what is to be. He lets the Lord and the Church determine the conditions, in such a way that his life acquires a countenance which is decisively formed in the Church's storehouse of graces—the Communion of Saints. The more he surrenders himself the more his natural face coincides with this supernatural countenance, which is more than just personal. His traits assume the stamp which the Church offers him from her position above time; but this "stamp" is by no means a mask, nor is it interchangeable, as if it could be fitted at will to this or that person. Rather, there takes place a fusion and interpenetration between an earthly and a heavenly countenance. What comes out of it is the result of the Church's fruitfulness, which rests on the double foundation of Mary's virginity and of the person who now is vowing virginity for the first time.

The Church, for whose life the sacrament of penance is so all-important, produced a Saint John Vianney in order to make clear with his example what the grace of confession is. He bears all the ideal traits of one who hears confessions, one who becomes intuitive through hearing confessions and is strengthened by his struggle with the forces of evil. But this can occur only by reason of his virginity and inviolability. His mission has its origin at the point where the priest is called by Christ as an individual to follow him to the Cross itself.

With his whole existence the priest stands between communion and confession, receiving and giving, knowing and believing, between acquired and ecclesial knowledge and an infused knowledge of sin. In the case of the priest, fruitfulness can almost be touched with one's hands, both that which he has acquired by his own fidelity and, at the same time, that with which the Church has chosen to distinguish him. For the Church does both things: it both confers distinction and exacts a life of distinction. The figure of John Vianney reveals the stamp which the Church has designed in advance. He identified himself with what the Church offered him in this design.

VIII

FAITH, PRAYER AND SACRAMENT

A father will allow his maturing child the freedom to converse with him at certain times in a completely unforced manner. During his time of work, he cannot let the child bother him at every moment, but in his free time he is at the child's disposal. The child can then tell him about things, pose questions, relate to him in all love's naturalness and communicate to him everything conceivable, either in a more or less orderly way or totally as it comes to him.

But then there is also the conversation that the father himself determines. He wants to tell the child something or ask him to account for this or that. He desires to supervise his child's progress and to observe what he has learned, what he thinks, and how he is developing. He wishes to enrich the child's education and experience with new knowledge and abilities. He himself determines the content of such an interchange and, therefore, also establishes the direction of the conversation. He has decided on a certain order to follow, and if he has been attentive to his child, he will be able to anticipate his answers for the most part. To certain questions he can expect certain answers that reveal the knowledge available to the child. In this he can be disappointed, both in the good and the bad sense. And the child, who relates to his father with love and respect, will enjoy this conversation conducted by the father. There are times, though, when he would rather engage in something more independent. At other times, he again longs for such a conversation, and he can hardly wait until his father has time to embark upon any subject he chooses.

Something similar happens with prayer. Just as the child must be ready at any time his father appoints, since the father plans his time as he will, so, too, does the one praying approach God knowing that God has the right to appoint times, as well as the right to choose a subject, to begin dialogue at a particular point, and to carry it on a given day this far and no further. The one praying knows that God does not have to take into account what he is feeling right now, or what desires he might have, or whether he would have gladly chosen the same subject. A readiness is here involved that cannot be procured through one's natural constitution and that is not available as a matter of course, but that must be acquired through a certain asceticism. Such an attitude of wanting to remain open, the kind of waiting that does not turn into a paralysis, requires a renunciation. A person will very consciously have to decide on those measures that are necessary in order for him to remain watchful according to the counsel of the Gospel. To achieve this, no rules may be devised that will be valid for everyone at all times. God has created both persons and situations to be very different. But the direction can be indicated by one's own experience and one's own prayer, by the rule, and by the knowledge and experience of others, especially that of one's confessor and spiritual director. The fact that advice is at all necessary likewise belongs to the ascesis. It belongs to the sacrifice and the renunciation into which the person wants to be initiated, and it belongs as well to the establishing and deepening of that *readiness* which the person at prayer seeks both in his actions and in his very being. In itself, however, readiness is not enough. Genuine readiness must be able to translate into action what is present in the person as a *habitus.* At God's request, readiness must become action, the consent must be uttered and prayer must be actualized.

But, just as the child does not limit his association with his father to those exchanges which the father himself regulates, so, too, does the one who prays not "acquit himself of God" when he has carried out those intervals of prayer appointed by God—whether the Liturgy of the Hours, private meditation or the exercises prescribed by the rule. The freedom of the one praying does not consist in not having to pray the rest of the time. A free space does, indeed, remain to him after prayer which is enjoined, but that, too, is a space for prayer. Prescribed prayer establishes a certain order that constitutes the asceticism of prayer: observing the Hours, organizing one's thoughts, keeping one's readiness lively—the right standards, in other words. Taking his cue from this order of things, the person is then free to shape his prayer as his heart dictates. But if those standards were wanting, his prayer would remain half-realized. It would lose a great share of immediacy and liveliness, thus "missing the mark". Such prayer would think it was attaining something which would, nevertheless, not be the precise thing God had determined for it. God is such a lover of order that His first deed was to order chaos. And so, what he desires above all in a person who relates to him is order: order in the service of prayer, an order that God himself establishes and in which a person ought to find his contentment. It is in the context of this order that God bestows freedom.

Order in prayer derives ultimately from the triune God. If God loves order so much it is because he possesses it in himself. The whole of his Trinitarian life rests on a fundamental order in the procession of the divine Persons and in their imperturbable relations with one another. God reveals this, his order, exteriorly, and man's participation in this order is called faith. And faith does not merely receive information, as it were, concerning the divine order; rather it is nourished by it, returning to it in prayer and in the activity of love that faith imparts to us—a return to the eternal and free life of Father, Son and Spirit.

When the Holy Spirit shows himself to us with his own properties—the seven gifts and fruits, which we can indeed count but not systematize—this corresponds to the whole of God's order. In this manner, God discloses something of the eternal order, so that man will have an opportunity to come nearer to it. This order, of course, persists not only at the moment when the Spirit discloses it, but just as much when it remains concealed. But in God concealment does not mean withdrawal of love and revelation, nor is it the opposite of God's self-disclosure. For this reason, man can have before God no other attitude but that of disclosure. A certain concealment is perhaps advisable with regard to one's fellow men and human institutions, but even this concealment will then be seen to derive from a final condition of being disclosed before God. Whoever desires to conceal something before God has forsaken the divine order of things. Man's order is always his manifestness before God, and this is the relationship God expects of believers, a relationship shown to be one of love. The child who hides something from his father knows that he has forsaken the order of things. And if the child at times hides something from his father in order to give him a surprise, he would not finally be disappointed if he found out that the father already knew about it. But such a game of hide-and-seek cannot exist where God is concerned. No one can say to God in prayer or in any other form of dialogue, "I'll answer you later. I'll show you some other time how I've planned my life, what I think of your wisdom and how I intend to keep your commands." Prayer is always a perfect and immediate self-disclosure, even if the one praying cannot produce a final, decisive word a human listener would expect, and this because a word of prayer may only be made to "rhyme" by God himself. Man has only to set out in a certain direction and God unfolds the way before him, the Way which he himself is.

The Church's coming into being may only be understood from the prayer of the Son. His word becomes deed, visible act. The result can, to a certain extent, be seen, but not wholly, of course. For, in his word and as Word, the Son remains the Word of the Father, and everything is thus prolonged into the invisible, directed towards the Father. The Son's word follows an orientation from earth to heaven, and it has its final reality there. To understand anything in our world we must compare it to the grain of mustard of the parable: something small—the smallest of all—is, indeed, grasped and understood, but only as something in the process of becoming, whose growth and fruit are of another world. This holds not only for the Church as a whole, but for each sacrament in particular. Faith can grasp a portion of the way, but then it is itself grasped by what is greater and invisible, and it can hardly keep up with this greater reality any longer. As a faith that can be understood, it is, with regard to what is actually occurring, but a small attempt to penetrate into the great model of faith, which is to say the divine understanding that exists among the three Persons. This it is that grasps the believer and which he can never grasp.

A Christian who brings his child to be baptized knows in faith the meaning of the sacrament. He understands that part which has been given him to understand, but in prayer he leaves the greater part of it to the Church and the triune God. A certain portion of prayer itself is evident to him. He knows why he kneels down before God and receives a sacrament, but he also knows that the knowledge he has in faith is infinitely surpassed by the divine knowledge of the Holy Spirit. Nothing is clearer to him than that his understanding can only take one step, and that he can never keep up with the content of his faith. And so the same asceticism is needed for everything: for his faith, for his prayer, for the reception of the sacraments—a continual act of saying Yes that encompasses the greater reality that is forever escaping him. For this, a certain discipline of spirit is indispensable that refrains from making faith and its effects fit the personal standards of one's intelligence and talents. The petty devotionalism we so often encounter in the Church and which makes faith out to be something nice and sentimental, thus making it appear ridiculous to others, has its constant basis in the attempt to confine the divine by the standards of the human. Here a person no longer stands before the face of his God, but before an image that he has carved for himself with his reason according to the standards of his own nature. Certain elements of that image may be true and genuine; but he has reduced them to the extent of totally dominating them, and has even perhaps made of his faith the perfect effigy of his own weaknesses, fears and limitations. And here the difference between talent and limitation is not so great, since they both have human bounds. A Christian can, for example, have his child baptized so that he will belong to the same community as his parents, but at the same time he might totally exclude from this event the boundless grace of God, and fail to place the child at God's free disposal. And yet, he should know that every sacrament not only contains the seed of freedom, but the full possibility of freedom's expansion, given to man by God. A sacrament is not only abundant in itself; it also has the effect of abounding in the believer. In order that this essential property of a sacrament might remain real, a person must always give his assent to that in him which is greater than he, and remain open to the demands of sacramental grace. This must be done not by approximation, shrugging one's shoulders and saying, "Maybe God will make something of it", but with an affirmation of God's greatness and with a surrender that implies that one does not want to supervise everything personally. The sacraments have a direction, but not a measure. For them to become fruitful, the believer must give up the conviction that he "knows better". He must stop designing plans and laying down lines of demarcation. He must allow the gratitude and devoted discipleship he possesses to develop with the freedom of the children of God. Within this development there is somewhere a leap that the striver will succeed in making only if he knows the meaning of renunciation and asceticism. In spite of his good will, he can come up against an obstacle that will disorient him for some time to come. He will then seem to be experiencing nothing but stagnation and to be walking around in circles. He has, in addition, been so accustomed to using his understanding for measuring, judging and criticizing things that a renunciation of this practice of setting up boundaries appears to him to be barely possible and, indeed, undesirable. Here only asceticism can help—the lively

coming to grips with the demand of faith to let God be
our truth and to let the paltry ramifications of human
order open out to God's greater and unsurveyable order.
By saying this, I am not advocating disorder in the
reception of the sacraments and in prayer. The sacraments bear an order in themselves. The order does not
lie with the receiver, but in the sacrament, and this
sacramental order corrects what in the receiver is dis-
ordered. Confession is the best example of this. We
confess our errors and, as we confess, they assume a
totally different import. Previously we had ourselves
determined that import, while confession relieves us of
its burden. We had fashioned a certain idea of what
redemption through absolution is all about, but it now
comes to us differently than expected. We had sketched
for ourselves the new start we would make after confession, but it could not quite be thought through,
since we can neither determine nor scrutinize grace in
advance. In this way, asceticism before the reception of
the sacraments consists of humility, simplicity and
childlikeness. The Lord's saying, "Let the children come
to me", is the way to the sacraments. But it is, nonetheless,
a way of the asceticism of the spirit. Now can the Lord
himself take up the child that comes to him. What he
does with him belongs to the Lord's providence. The
Lord will bestow on him that form of spirituality that
will, in him, correspond to the Holy Spirit's action, and
this gift will enable the believer to give his answer to
the Spirit. The answer itself will be the encounter of the
sacrament received with the truth of all sacraments in

God's own hand. As something received by man, the sacrament now stands over against God's totality. While the believer is not *himself* communion, through the communion he receives he nevertheless corresponds to the great "order of communion" in God. Likewise, he is not *himself* confession; but, as one who confesses, he belongs to the "order of confession" in God. No equation of believer and sacrament takes place here, rather an encounter of both orders, that of God and that of the believing person. And, in the sacraments, it is God himself who creates the basis and sets the stage for such an encounter.

In John's opening phrase, "In the beginning was the Word, and the Word was with God", the Word's "being with God" at the same time indicates its standpoint and its attitude. It has taken its stand with God and cannot be moved from this location. It has been there from the beginning. Neither our coming to the Word, nor our contemplation of it, nor our struggles with it, nor even our submission to it can alter anything about the Word's standpoint. Whatever is with God remains with him, and only from there does it have its effects. It does not have to return constantly to its point of departure in order to acquire new power and meaning: it always possesses these in all their fullness there where it is.

The Word is obedient to the Father, and for our sake he becomes ascetical. As soon as he becomes for us the Word of Revelation, as soon as he includes us in his own obedience, we must become ascetics for the sake of that obedience. We can come close to him only through the asceticism that he gives us, an asceticism that is already found in his obedience by way of an example. The asceticism of the Word is a gift of grace which invites us, brings us back, leads us from a standpoint within ourselves to *his* standpoint in God. Insofar as we are being *led,* our transformation is effected by him; we have only to add our consent, a consent which hardly holds any weight but which is nonetheless a condition. Yet this very condition has already been permanently fulfilled by the unconditionality with which the Son bows to the Father. "Perhaps", "tomorrow" and "later" are words which cannot even be considered. Everything must always be "today". The exterior circumstances of our life, its human frailty and inconstancy, do not at all change the fact that the action must be accomplished in the present and that the unconditional Yes must be uttered today. It seems almost unbelievable that a human being should be asked to perform an unconditional action, and yet not so unbelievable, since this action is already contained in God's own unconditionality. As he does it, a person remains what he is: the creature that abides in the Father's act of creation and yet who can make his own decisions, who can be a friend of God and yet shrink back with fear before him, and who can erect obstacles and walls that make the continuing advance of grace impossible for the time being. But a person realizes that things cannot proceed in this way. The Yes that has once been uttered must demolish the walls of finitude in order to find the place that belongs to it within the Father's unconditionality. Capitulation and surrender to the Word occur precisely where one has failed and has run into an impasse. The oppressive experience of finitude whets the edge of asceticism, giving it a contour and revealing it as the means necessary for persevering in one's consent. Much can be taken back, but never one's consent. Taking it back would separate the creature from its Creator as if it had fallen from his hand.

All things have been created for the Son, even man and his consent. By giving his consent, a person shows he is filling with meaning the fact that he has been predetermined by the Father for the Son. Even as one existing in this world, he has been created for a world where he can belong to the Son. By giving his assent, he can let God shape his life in this world in such a way that the fact of his being created for that other world comes to prevail. In this way, a truth of the infinite God can become visible to his fellow humans and to the Church through one small human act of renunciation.

The first human couple spoke with God in intimacy. Distance between them came about through sin. Sin alienated man, and his dialogue with God became exposed to every manner of confusion. God's Word was misunderstood or not heard at all or heard at the wrong place; questions and answers were no longer adequate to one another. Only the Cross makes genuine dialogue possible once again, and this through the existence of the Church. The Church takes up man's word and carries it before God, and through the Gospel she conveys to the one praying the certainty that he is being heard. She also mediates God's Word and guidance in their full unconditionality. The Church thus plays the role of an "exchange", a place where a conversation is received and regulated. The ascetical aspect of such an arrangement consists above all in man's no longer having an excuse for misunderstanding the Word. The Word has been "registered" and "entered in": it can be scrutinized within the confines of the Church. This possibility forces a person to restructure his attitude, allowing the Church to examine what God expects of him by way of asceticism. Such an examination of things belonging to the Bride attains, through the Bride, to the Bridegroom. The Bride cannot stop offering the Bridegroom her children's gifts or what the saints produce in the Church's communion. Their consent becomes a gift of the Church to her Lord. The Church unites this gift to the "Word that is with God" in a returning movement that reaches the very beginning, discloses the ways of Providence and gives the individual who experiences something of this a feeling of strange solitude and yet also of community, since what he experiences is also experienced by every other believer. He thus utters his Yes to the community that, in the Word, has been chosen from the beginning, and yet for him the sound of this Yes somehow lacks an echo, as if it had been uttered in a vacuum without the earthly assurance that his renunciation, his self-disclosure before God or his surrender have been really accepted. He intended all of this for God, and what he encounters is the Church. But he knows that, likewise, when he aimed for the Church, he had encountered God. And he knows that it belongs to his renunciation, as well as to the core of his faith, to integrate his word into God's Word through the Church.

IX

THE READING OF SACRED SCRIPTURE

Christian asceticism is a living process that involves the whole person and aids him in effecting time and again the proper unity that ought to exist between body and soul, between God's question and man's answer. In this process there is no room for hesitations, complaints or postponements. The demand is urgent and the answer must follow at once. The attitude, therefore, that results from an ascetical will is a firm one, a clearly enunciated and distinctly realized Yes. But asceticism is itself an attitude which is received from the Word. Sacred Scripture constantly calls a person to adopt such an attitude. He reads, for instance, how the Lord is tired and the crowds, nevertheless, leave him no rest—so great is their desire to hear him and see his miracles. He reads how the apostles on the Mount of Olives fall asleep in spite of the Lord's request and are unable to achieve what is asked of them. Or he reads the Lord's words concerning fasting or how the Lord is scourged or how the apostles experience fear on the stormy lake. By means of all this, the Scripture not only wants to educate us in a limited human sense; it wants to reach us with the total claim that only God's Word can make. Although a human kind of education is not excluded, it is our word of surrender in faith that Scripture is after.

It accompanies the believer through all dangers of his everyday life, through all promising as well as all hesitating, in order to lead him to the Lord. The word of Scripture is such a living reality that it returns unswervingly to the one from whom it originated. Scripture encloses the believer, as it were, like an armor that is stronger than he is and which protects him, making him invulnerable to danger; but occasionally it adjusts so tightly that it hurts and even wounds him. An armor possesses its own form, leaving room here but fitting there much too snugly. The pressure can be so much that it first causes pain, then a wound appears and finally perhaps even a permanent sore. Whoever accommodates himself to the Word, making his own form pliant, finds himself protected and firmly bolstered by it. It chastises only the recalcitrant, and for him it does become an unbearable burden.

But an individual cannot look at Scripture only through the eyes of his own faith. He is, of course, guided by it; but, in itself, Scripture was entrusted by the Lord to his Bride, the Church. The inspiration that impelled the Evangelists to take pen in hand continues to illumine the Church. The Church is inspired by Scripture; she mediates the Scripture, accompanying it with her tradition, fostering commentaries on it and making it the chief matter of her instruction. It goes without saying that Scripture will always contain more than is actually brought to light by interpretations. But the Church supervises very closely the manner of the Scripture's use. Persons committed to the Church—priests and religious—keep watch over the Scriptures and administer the precious treasure entrusted to them, having the obligation of passing it on to believers as their new life. The situation is, therefore, not one where the believers are on one side, with all their enthusiasms and personal opinions, with an endless variety of ideas and all the ups and downs of their energies and involvements, while on the other side is the Scripture, waiting to be tugged and interpreted every which way according to the enthusiasm present, something out of which one may take what one needs and ignore what does not gratify. Scripture constitutes an indivisible whole, and no one will ever exhaust its full sense. When a person seriously considers a passage of Scripture, he must relate it to the whole, since no passage stands alone but rather is connected with all the others in a living and organic manner. A word is but a dry sign on a piece of paper; but the Word is also God, and from each word of Scripture an infinite projection opens out, reaching to God's total fullness. Conversely, everything that God gives us can be concentrated in a single word of Scripture. But a word of Scripture can no more be isolated from all the rest than an organ can exercise its own function when it has been isolated from the other organs. A word of Scripture exists only in relation, in the living context of God with his faithful in the Church, in Christ, and in the totality of creation and redemption. And a word of Scripture is always there to serve: anyone can reach for it and put it to use to achieve an integration into the whole.

Essentially, the Word is nothing but an ever-flowing gift.

The fact that the word of Scripture is at the same time both individual reality and contextual reality sheds new light on the whole ascetical attitude of the Christian. He cannot be partial to one form of asceticism and reject the others. He cannot, for instance, select certain penitential exercises which he is willing to perform and decline others. He is present to the whole Word and must also consider himself a whole ordered to God, living in a unity of body and spirit. Such unity is nourished and fostered by his answer to the ascetical demands of Scripture, demands that are always meant personally. In every instance, the choice of a correct form of asceticism will follow the universal law of Christian choice: a person chooses God in order to make himself available to *God's* choice. When he offers something to God, he will, therefore, attempt to offer everything he is, so as to leave the choice up to God. The believer resembles an organ with many registers. It is God's affair on which register he plays now and on which he plays later, so as to produce the melody and harmony he intends. It could appear that certain registers are never used, as if they were totally forgotten, and then suddenly they are very much brought into play. When a responsible person allows himself a great freedom of decision in his worldly and Christian life, he ought not forget how much more freedom the Lord of all possesses in comparison with him. The one who has gladly played subject must also gladly desire to be the object of God's perfect play.

Time and again a person will find himself at the end of his rope, and only the Lord can turn this situation into a new beginning. Peter and his friends fish the entire night without catching anything. Or the disciples quarrel with one another for the first place without arriving at a solution. Or Peter denies the Lord three times and even his tears cannot undo what he has done. On every side the disciples come up against the unresolvable and work themselves into desperate situations. And every time it is the Lord's appearing, his intervening, that brings the solution, an overflowing solution of grace.

And so the Christian who was supposed to follow the Lord finds himself in a kind of no-exit consisting of doubt, hesitation, anguish and the inability to understand. And he does not possess the courage necessary to engage his faith fully, a faith that contains the solution: namely, to concede the Lord and his Word the full claim they have. For the same reason, he does not have the courage to admit to himself fully the gap that exists between his present attitude and faith's ideal. And yet, both things must again coincide. In the Gospel, such coincidence occurs when the Lord intervenes. It does not say that this was always desired by the apostles whenever they did not obey or became entangled in their discussions and conflicts. In an obscure way they know that, when the Lord's grace is granted and the question is resolved, they themselves will be shown to be in the wrong. By showing them how conscious he has been the whole time of their needs and cares, the Lord exacts of them a kind of involuntary confession necessary for absolution. Through the grace of confession, they become conscious that they have failed, conscious of how much more they ought to have relied on the Lord and of how they should have expected infinitely more from him. The word of the Lord draws this awareness out of the blockage of a bad conscience where it lay hidden. The fact that it must be freed implies a new form of asceticism for the Christian. He must subordinate his "knowing better" to the Lord's truly better wisdom, and this does not result in servitude, but in a liberation to true freedom. Because obedience has no room for reservations, obedience to the Word places a person before the ever-greater, ever-truer reality of the Lord. This means, however, that obedience likewise has no room for the limitations of a personal ego whose self-denial and renunciation is expected to be perfect. Such self-denial can only be perfect when a person *allows* God to take from him what he must. Everytime he says *I* or *mine* or speaks from an experience that involves him totally he nevertheless knows that grace has objectively already overtaken all of this. When he now says "I", he can no longer mean the "I" he himself intends, but only the "I" that the Lord intends and which is, therefore, totally different. It is a much greater "I", since grace inhabits it, and a much broader "I", because the Lord has made so many of his divine and human mysteries abide with it.

When someone prays in faith, he is accustomed to address the heavenly Father without possessing too clear-cut an idea of him. In faith a person can assert many things about God in ever-new ways, but this does not keep his concept of God from remaining wholly mysterious, not to be defined in human ways. In order to venture an address to God at all, a totality of faith is still needed with all those dimensions that transcend human consciousness. Just as faith and prayer gravitate toward this sphere of mystery and must nourish themselves on mystery in order to derive their Christian sense from it, so too must Christian asceticism be constructed on the foundation of mystery, bringing mystery into play and having to deal with it without, nevertheless, being able to encompass it at will. This sphere of mystery is the Lord himself—his Word and his grace. It is the sphere of his divine freedom, which stands at no one's disposal and which itself disposes of men.

Asceticism for a Christian can thus never become exhausted through a moralistic fulfillment of duties. To be sure, asceticism involves a giving of answers, self-exertion and discipline on the part of man: it is an experience *he* makes. But, at the same time, it is an intervention of forces over which God alone rules. A healthy person knows approximately how much fatigue he can endure, how far he can run, or how high he can climb. He is equal to these exertions. It could be that on some hike he will one day have to achieve more than foreseen: he has to return in the cold and the fog or he hurts himself or his food runs out—and he can do it. But these extra exertions still lie within certain boundaries. It could also be that he achieves less than he had intended, and this "less" also has its boundaries. In Christian asceticism, however, the "more" that lies in God becomes an incalculable magnitude. A person cannot know how much God will himself provide. But, on undertaking discipleship, a person must know what he himself is expected to provide. He must have faith, must persevere and must show a certain proficiency in whatever field it might be. He must not be constantly discouraged, full of hesitations and getting caught up in petty trains of thought that always have him jumping out of his skin and making himself a nuisance. He must first sit down and, as the Lord says, "take stock". But this calculation remains open in an upward direction. He has surrendered himself wholly, but he does not know what this "wholly" implies. No one who achieves total surrender possesses a comprehensive view of its expanse. It is as if he were to require the assent of his interior reality, a reality of which he has about as much *experience* as he does of the inner organs of his body. And it is not his consent that awakens these unconscious elements to consciousness but the call of God, who suddenly wants to hold sway over something in him he did not even know existed. By being called, these organs of the spirit become animated and, in their awakening, they gain in familiarity and are cherished, but perhaps only in order to be sacrificed and surrendered. Other organs awaken only to become a burden. Sacrifices are now expected, and the renouncing of things that until now did not even have a name; dispositions and character traits must now be surrendered which had never come to light. Pain and joy now intermingle in new ways, in order that the person might truly awaken and his surrender be genuine in every direction, in order that his consent might come to encompass things which he never consciously intended. For the Lord wishes those who give themselves to him to experience a fullness of joy.

When the disciples went about with the Lord on earth, observing him and seeking to draw their conclusions, he was always there to answer their questions. And his answers were so fashioned that they could understand and meditate them, but at the same time they realized that his answers were considerably greater than their questions, that he offered them more than they had expected, and that he even knew what their dormant needs were, caring for them through his Word in advance. And he did this in an abundant measure. The disciples were in need of an asceticism of the spirit in order to receive the Word as it was being uttered. They had to tame their impatience, put a rein on their impulse to question and on their thirst for instruction, in order to accept step by step, day by day, what was offered to them. Something of this must come to life in everyone who reads the Scriptures. He knows they are inspired, and he suspects the great correspondences they contain, the presence in them of the most profound truths and the abundance of their Christian teachings. In many places he sees heaven stand open and send down an enticing ray of its glory. But a human being cannot live in continual ecstasy or think constantly of eternity. The substance of contemplation must include the terrestrial and the present in a kind of analogy to the Incarnation. It must be content with what is small even when something great could practically be grasped, and it must also be able to detach itself even from what is small when this is demanded, thus remaining open for both extremes and everything in between.

In this way, even that which appears to be most insignificant, the tiniest word in Scripture — an *and* or a *but* — can be pondered for a long time. It will always yield new connections, transitions and lasting truths. The Bible possesses a fundamental character that permeates the whole of it, so that one can consider individual sentences, or then again whole stories, whether the text appears to be quite definitive and conclusive or, on the contrary, open and overpowering. The one meditating the Scriptures must educate his spirit to attain an elastic availability, as it were, which on the one hand abandons all barriers and on the other can accept clear boundaries. He must learn at one moment to jump over confinements, and at another moment to let himself be contained by them even when the hedge seems to be quite low. And all of this occurs out of obedience to the Scripture, to the Lord, to the Church and the order. Then will the truth that is granted unfold in its variety of aspects, and it will exhibit its power in every spirit that does not become arrogant and wishes to be ascetical and obedient. The difficulties of the contemplative life can become very great, but these are difficulties proper to asceticism, which is to say difficulties that God places as obstacles and hurdles and that keep asceticism from becoming a routine and obedience from becoming a habit. In Christianity, nothing ought to collect rust; everything should constantly be so shot through with the Lord's life that the one praying experiences this life as a source, a mountain spring, a rebirth of things which just yesterday he knew nothing about, even if he should already have lived in the order for twenty years. Expressions such as, "I've already gotten the picture", or "I've already been through that", or "There's nothing new for me", are statements that have no place in asceticism. Both priests and religious have, of course, had their experiences. But the evolving current of the life of grace is stronger still. More than others is such a one called to expand himself. For him more than for others should each word of the Lord be a new Word.

X

OUR NEIGHBOR

In the daily involvement with other persons, everyone obeys certain laws. These are as varied as human faces. Many laws arise on the spot, others are traditional, others still are hardly defined and nevertheless demand in a strict and inexorable manner that they be obeyed. Some laws are established by self-interest, others derive from the area of morality, others simply make a given way of life run smoothly and they are binding for those involved. Many of these laws have nothing to do with asceticism, since they are so loose-fitting and so coincide with people's desires that they are as flexible as life itself. Man makes a law valid for himself out of whatever is convenient for him.

Whoever lives "ascetically" in the Christian sense possesses an interior rule that gives expression to Christianity, a rule whose contents aim at Christian goals and which have no objective but providing Christian discipleship with a palpable countenance. This "rule" is, therefore, born of the Lord's Word; it is pliant to the Lord and acknowledges his power as law-giver. The person who makes this rule his own is aware not only of the fact that countless others before him have done the same thing, but that, beyond this, he has the evidence of the Church's experience before him, and that, in this way, any fundamental error is excluded, since Christian asceticism is a part of Christian truth. But it can happen that on comparing this rule with his own inclinations, a person will shrink back because of its rigor, and he will think of the whole enterprise as being unrealizable, not believing that this road will take him anywhere. If, against his expectations, however, things should proceed fairly well, he then runs the danger of becoming arrogant and of flaunting his "strength" before those who have faltered on the road or those who have given up in spite of their faith. He becomes haughty, and increasingly so in proportion to the number of things he has overcome or the degree to which he has lived "ascetically".

Such arrogance destroys the whole edifice of asceticism, turning it into a school of the devil. And suddenly we see in a new light the little man who had given up the race, finding the task too difficult and not having enough courage to struggle earnestly with the demands of Christ. Now we see that he possesses a humble honesty which the ascetic lacked. Arrogance can obviously not be the result of asceticism. Asceticism must develop out of humility in the first place, and, if it is found to be genuine and truthful, it must initiate a person trying to overcome himself into an ever-growing humility. He will then recognize his limitations and appraise his insufficiency. He will continually come up against the resistance of his ego and its need for comfort. He will not be satisfied, even when his accomplishments in fact coincide with the Commandments and obedience is strictly carried out. This is so because Christian revelation and Christian asceticism together form a unity. The humble person will, therefore, have to be constantly reborn through asceticism. Over and over again he will return to the very fountainhead of Christianity in order to experience what is discipleship, what obedience, what penance, and this not in his own imagination but in the sense conferred by Christ. More and more he is "tuned into" the Lord's sense, and nothing remains to him but to be humble. He can now assign no values and standards to himself. Values and standards lie in the rule, which is to say in the Lord's hand. It is the *Lord's* judgment that decides. The Christian who accomplishes great things at whatever level of asceticism can never ascribe his achievements to himself, but only to the fact that the Lord and his grace have entrusted him with a task. Asceticism thus makes a Christian into a *thankful* person. Thankfulness and love must spontaneously flow out of him if his asceticism is to bear the sign of genuineness. If they should be lacking we can be sure that an all-too-human element has crept in and that guilt and aberrations are not far off. To be sure, no one who considers taking up the way of the Lord's Cross to the extent demanded of him will, for the moment, show signs of irrepressible joyfulness. But in spite of the Lord's suffering and that which is enjoined on him, he will be at peace, and he will radiate something of the truth of revelation, a truth perceived in peace. And this will occur so visibly that he himself will appear to become a fountain of truth, not for himself (for his glance is fixed on the Lord), but for his fellow men.

Something can appear to one person to demand great efforts which, for another, happens quite naturally, since it seems to him to be the obvious consequence of something he has understood. Perhaps he does it so spontaneously because it appears as the only thing to do. The first person, however, will constantly feel that he is being "jabbed", as it were, by the ascetical rule as by a goad from the outside. In all this he can never come to forget about himself. But this difference among persons, however, is in itself no reason for worry. The difference of reaction is, in fact, the case with every virtue, every act of obedience, even with every prayer and dialogue with God. One person is consumed with the impatience of finally being allowed to do this or that ascetical work, while another person finds the burden so great that he needs to muster the effort of all his forces in order just to "hang on". Whatever the case may be, the Christian never lives following a rule which has either been self-invented or agreed to by a collectivity. He lives on the Word of the Lord, a Word which makes it possible in the first place for him to encounter his fellow man as a *neighbor* in the Lord's sense, and to mediate to this neighbor what is the Lord's. He lives in a humility that makes him bow down before the gift of grace he is supposed to radiate.

The form of love that the Lord chose for our redemption is the Cross. The Father had held the hour back until the last moment, and then gave it full power. On the Mount of Olives, the Son prays that the cup might pass from him. The cup contains the suffering; it has a definite form and a definite content which must be emptied out in all its bitterness. The Son takes up form and content in a way corresponding to his mission. That the cup must be drained to the last drop means for him that he must give his life away to the extreme and with much pain for the redemption of the world. Indissoluble connections are here present: between God and man, between the Son and sinners, between his atoning suffering and our guilt. The Son gives his life to the Father for mankind, and, by fulfilling the Father's will, he is open in his suffering to mankind. The two beams of the Cross are a symbol of this double movement: a symbol which, in the hour of the Cross, becomes perfect reality. His death is now as real as his life ever was, and both of them out of love. Death is surrender, renunciation, emptying out until nothing remains. Life had been love, fullness, dialogue.

Both extremes of death and life are to be found in every genuine form of Christian asceticism, as well as the law of vicarious representation: suffering before God for mankind. This, too, is shown by the intersecting beams which, ever since they came together in the Cross, can no longer be separated. An asceticism directed only to God, a purely vertical asceticism, is unthinkable in a Christian sense. The chief commandment, encompassing the love of God and of neighbor, can never be only half-fulfilled. The Cross is the form of every Christian ascesis, precisely in its vicarious double movement: toward God and for men.

The person engaged in prayer or in penance or in

self-surrender is, indeed, striving after God; but in the midst of his striving he even forgets about his road out of his love for his neighbor. He loses sight of himself as a striver in order to find the countenance of his fellow men. Even the person who enters a contemplative monastery, only to pray and atone, will in this activity have his neighbor before his eyes, trying to help him along in his following of the crucified Lord. His goal is God, but he is implanted on the Cross in order to receive there what the Son intends for him—whatever has the form of the Cross. The two beams together form an unalterable angle, not an angle of harmony, but one of firmly established contradiction. The scales comprised by the horizontal beam may not be loaded one-sidedly, since the vertical beam must point directly to the Father. But once the vertical becomes an essential part of the Cross, then the place for the horizontal is already present, prepared for in advance and immovable.

And yet, whoever has chosen this way cannot simply set himself on the Cross, extend his arms and somehow remain idle, enduring whatever may come over him. He must, rather, search out his way in an active surrender, until he has wholly forgotten about himself and is nothing but a tool, not only of each beam, but of Christ's Cross, at last an instrument in the Father's hands. A person cannot himself *become* the Cross; he can only suffer some part of it. He does not *become* the Cross anymore than he *becomes* obedience. A certain place has been set aside for him. Providence knows what awaits him and is destined for him. He must bear and *be borne* by prayer as a natural medium. His own prayer is a part of it, but anonymously; most important is the prayer of his brethren, of the Church, the prayer of sinners that are counting on redemption. The form of asceticism can thus not be chosen ultimately, since it has always been there. And if a person wanted to atone for a specific sin, for a sinner personally known to him, for an event he wants to avert, he can do this only in the horizontal form that continues infinitely and disappears from sight, the form which encompasses one's fellow men, among them also the person who had been expressly intended. But his prayer also encompasses persons he had not intended, sins which seemed to him to be too abhorrent, all sins, in fact, even those whose names he ignores. The event that alarmed him is included, but also all past and future events that alarm others, even those events that God will not admit, because he grants this prayer the efficacy and the power promised by the Son himself, who said that prayer can move mountains.

Someone who had meditated much about it could say the subtlest things about self-surrender and find in his prayer the most unique words to express his meaning. All of these words would nevertheless already be contained in the form of the Cross and would have to be able to be traced back to it. That which is subtle and hardly effable suddenly receives the roughest and simplest appearance: a cross raised up on a hill so that it can be seen from afar. No member of an order can count on a cross of his own or on a form of suffering agreeable to him—whatever it may be—not even a personal form of suffering. He is of those who belong to the Cross, a cross which is widely visible and easy to describe, almost anonymous, since only the name of the crucified Lord is unique. The one who sacrifices himself casts into this name everything which for him had hitherto possessed a name and a form. Whoever knows "from the outside" that somewhere there is a place of the highest asceticism— for instance, a Carmelite monastery—really only needs to know no more about it than the fact that there the Cross is to be found. The asceticism of the person undertaking discipleship within the monastery should remain as anonymous as was the knowledge concerning asceticism of the person who still was on the outside. He undertakes such asceticism not for himself, but for his fellow men who care nothing about it and have perhaps never even heard of a life of asceticism, or for those who were once called and then became unfaithful, and for all the lukewarm who are as anonymous in the Church as the anonymity of those persons that are taken up by the Cross—anonymous, but in grace, anonymous within a light that stems from God and which replaces every name.

Asceticism is an attitude with regard to God and the world, but an attitude extended over the course of time. It is continuity: the individual ascetical act loses its sense when it does not derive from constancy and flow back into it. The one who prays does not only stand within ephemeral time looking at eternity. His time is equally a Christian time that encompasses what has been and what is to be. Its roots reach back to the first days of the world and only its fruits pass over into eternity. At a deeper level, time is extension and duration of eternity *over* worldly time, for without this accompaniment by eternal time, worldly time would have lost its meaning. An isolated act may be seen as a signal; but its full significance accrues to it only when it is seen as one of many, like a soldier in his rank within the army, only when it passes over into the anonymity of all other acts. An isolated act can be a sign of asceticism itself, but above all it is a sign of all who pray, a sign of the Church bound for God. It can be heroic and bear something unique about it, but it must itself *be borne* by all other acts. Otherwise, it loses its entire substance and, through this loss, enters a condition of total "lostness". It is stripped of its meaning. The Lord prefigured this state of affairs by living a life oriented toward the Cross, in such a way that all his words and deeds had a continuous significance and interconnection by which the uniqueness of the Cross was borne, a significance which gave meaning to the Cross and interpreted it. The Lord's Cross and life at the same time stand in continuity with eternal life, so that eternal life, too, might not lose its connection with asceticism from the Church's viewpoint. Eternal life disowns no one who prays, none of his prayers, not a single one of his acts. Much that appears incomprehensible in an earthly sense, because seen without any interconnection, receives its full meaning once it is seen as standing in a relationship to eternity.

We can see, then, that the asceticism of the individual is bound up, through time, with the life of all other men, whether they themselves perform ascetical acts and adopt an ascetical attitude or not. If someone, for instance, desired to salvage his spiritual and bodily life through some form of ascesis and, in so doing, thought only of himself, that asceticism would be alienated from its own sense. The person would be performing an act of self-seeking, an act of isolation and, therefore, of negation. Affirmation lies in being anonymous, in the acceptance of all men, in responsibility for them: in love. Through another's word a person can be brought to belief; he can be brought to reflect on faith and on his own ascetical attitude, and then, suddenly, grace will allow him to make the decision of letting everything happen as God wills it. The word that set all of this off appeared quite insignificant. It was probably spoken without much reflection, and perhaps it was even intended for someone else and was heard only by chance. But Providence had planned it so. The one who through this word attained to a new faith, however, will feel obligated to the person who uttered it, and he will incorporate him into his love and gratitude, and not only him, but everyone who by means of a word, a book or an attitude gave him what he needed in order to achieve a certain contemplative reflection and, thus, attain to asceticism. Whoever practices asceticism knows that he not only lives from grace as such, but that he lives from the manifold particular forms that grace assumes in other persons. Because he himself *bears,* he

knows that he *is borne;* because he strives *to love,* he
knows that he *is loved.* His fellow man is close to him,
the sinner as much as the saint. He experiences the
Communion of Saints, but also the life of non-Christians
and of those of different beliefs—in a word, the life of
all who are distant from him. He knows men precisely
insofar as they are *fellow* men, in the widest, most
human sense. And, since nothing human is foreign to
humans, he lives in a *state of being borne:* everyone is his
brother, he communicates his experience to him and
shares something of it with him, and this communicating and sharing occur in the grace and love of the
triune God, as a resonance of what, in God, is the
reality of several Persons having their Being in the one
Substance.

A mother who loves her small child has to carry it,
first physically within herself and then in her arms. She
nourishes it physically and spiritually, and when she
begins to speak with the child she must provide both
question and answer. As the child matures, it becomes
steadily more independent in its person and in its answers,
without the love and unity that exist between it and its
mother having thereby to decrease. In God, we must be
able to imagine the deepest unity of Being as being
intrinsically bound up with the highest development of
the Persons. Both the earthly likeness and the divine
model throw light on the life of grace as lived by the
ascetical Christian. He *bears,* but only by being funda-
mentally *borne along.* He takes a clearly defined stance
from which his life radiates out to his fellow men and to

God, and yet he is affected by both of these. He is supported by God and men; but, in order to be supported, he must be ascetical, and in order to be ascetical he must give himself away. What supports him, then, is receptiveness: the constant receiving of the grace that allows him to give himself away. The place where he is supported is ultimately a place where God and his fellow men encounter one another, a place for the encounter of the Bridegroom and the Bride. Asceticism is one moment within a constantly occurring dialogue.

The individual walks the road of asceticism as a mission, as the answer to a question. But the place where he stands is determined by God and the Church. An individual might think that by his prayer, his asceticism, his total attitude or by the sum of his attitudes, he somewhere defines a clear figure which, although not immediately visible to him, nevertheless stands on firm ground and has a definite road before it. But it is not like this. The road of asceticism is something like a state of suspension in which a person is at each step determined by the manner in which he is borne along by God and his fellow man. An ascetical person has lost his self-determination; he cannot even determine the content of his prayer, or the way his day is divided up, or the forms of his asceticism. This holds even where everything seems to be predetermined by the rule of an order, when a person takes on and performs a certain kind of penance, the Liturgy of the Hours or some responsibility of the apostolate. But the content of the exercise, the prayer and the action is at each moment determined anew by God along with the Church's cooperation. The more a person advances, the more developed and unbounded does the influence of these "determinants" become. In his prayer, the beginner thinks he can anticipate God's words, as a child who was good can anticipate his mother's praise: "You must be really happy now since I was so good!" The longer he continues in the ascetical life, the more surely he knows that what could be called God's "reaction" is unpredictable, and that neither the limits of his demands nor their nature can be established. Ultimately, this quality of "being Other" always adds to God's greater glory. A person, then, must always extend further those surfaces where he may be "gripped" by God and the Church, and in this extending of himself he must assume an attitude that will allow God, like a potter, to take his clay out of what appear to be definite forms and mold it into new and unsuspected shapes, until it becomes fully evident that a Christian can do nothing for himself, that everything has been left up to God and that he can give only because he receives.

XI

ECCLESIAL LOVE

The Son's presence to the Father during the entire course of his earthly life is a sign for us of his filial love, surrender and readiness. This love for the Father is not to be separated from his love for men. And, as if his love had not yet exhausted all its possibilities, the Son in the end founds the Church and raises her to the status of his Bride. In all three relationships he manifests his love. He does not reveal it conclusively, as if it were a wall that showed his accomplishments in engravings. Nor does he do it as in a mirror in which his efficacy could be seen as an image. Christ shows his love as being contained in the word that he is, as being opened through this word and as passing over into a silence that itself is love. But word, silence and his entire being are love, not only a love that gives, but also a love that always receives: an exchange. It is like a great circulatory system in which all flowing, throbbing and rushing is nothing but love. No unit or partial dependency may be dissociated from all others, and this total interconnectedness is itself a new proof of love.

This love is not there merely to be contemplated for its marvels—unless we finally give the word "contemplation" its full sense. One contemplates in order to become useful, in order to receive and to pass on, in order to learn the one thing necessary and to pass it on as such. Once contemplation acquires this sense, its absolute urgency becomes evident; we must at once see and understand—as far as we can understand—in order to give what we have perceived! If this must be done quickly, as quickly as possible, it is not because the Lord's image otherwise fades away, or because he shows us something only for an instant, but because so much time is always being lost: we have been loved for so long without realizing it, and we have loved for so long without allowing our love its full capacity.

Perhaps the greatest feat of the Lord's love was the founding of the Church. He chooses his Bride and allows each one of us to become representatives of this Bride. In our surrender to the Lord, each one of us can become his Bride, a Bride in and through the Church, as a response to the Lord's love for the Church. The thought that the Lord so loves me as an individual that I can become his Bride will sound wholly unbelievable to a person aware of the distance between a sinner and God. And yet, nothing is more real than the fact that we, unworthy though we are, are invited to partake in the love-relationship between Bride and Bridegroom. We are being awaited, since our invitation has been so urgent.

The Lord anticipated our helplessness by establishing the sacraments. He thus provided the Church with tokens of a fulfilled life. The decisive thing is, not that we are insufficiently prepared for it, but that the fullness of life is there—for us—and in such abundance that it covers everything like a flood and draws us into itself in spite of our impoverishment. If we were to evaluate a sacrament according to the dearth we bring with us, we could only stand there helplessly in our shame. But the shame should overpower us, at the most, for a very brief instant. For the fullness is there, independently of us: the Lord himself is this fullness. The sacraments do not border on one another like objects or substances that exhibit an edge and a limit. Each sacrament is "borne" by the Lord in the moment that he bestows it, in such a way that its union with the Lord and his fullness is achieved. And we receive what is offered us by way of fullness. Our imperfection cannot put a limit to it. We must avoid letting our finitude and limitations set themselves up *against* this fullness as a polarity. This could only have the effect of our not being wholly open to the fullness.

There are sacraments that are for everyone, and sacraments that are only for certain individuals. But even this is not a limitation, since every sacrament is, in itself, perfect. The totality of the faithful and individuals within this totality partake of the Lord in a manner providentially established by him—not on account of their obedience, but because of *his*. Thus we have an asceticism of the sacraments, but it is not an achievement of our own which we bring with us to the sacraments, rather a participation in the Lord's own ascesis which is bestowed on us. Before the Lord's ascesis we must bend the knee and accept it as it is. We must utter our Yes in imitation of the Mother who puts herself at the disposal of a Son who is blazing his way through her. For the Son, our consent will always echo something of his Mother's consent and thereby participate in its fullness. One sign of his acceptance of her consent is that he continues to listen for it as it resounds from us. He hears it even though our voice utters it faint-heartedly, and in this way he shows that his characteristic quality of being ever greater than we determines even his attitude toward us. He hears the whole of what we intend to say when we have hardly brought ourselves to stutter. The fullness of his Mother's consent becomes the Church's own consent, becomes the adequate answer of mankind to his own obedient Yes to the Father, a consent which is the source of all asceticism. His asceticism is identical with his love for God and men: it is only *we* who make the concept so narrow. And, just as this love expresses itself in the self-forgetfulness of the Cross, so, too, is it expressed in the surrender to service which he has made an essential part of his Church's manner of dispensing the sacraments, none of which is allowed by him to be jeopardized by our own failures. The receiver of a sacrament, therefore, has but one thing to do: through the Church's own consent, which derives from Mary's, he must open himself to the fullness of the Lord's love. Then will his faltering Yes pass over into the fullness of the sacraments, in order to be received and accepted there again with a truth and a final validity which the Lord himself guarantees. The person may still be so burdened with his own doubts and problems that he can hardly see a clear road ahead of him; his failures can bring him to almost total collapse, and, out of sheer helplessness, he may not know which way to turn. In the sacrament, nevertheless, every question has been overtaken in advance: it has been solved ecclesially, in a universal sense. Whatever the one praying may introduce into his prayer, even if it concerns the future, we may say that, in the sacrament, it is only a remembering. This "remembering" is in God himself; in the book of life and of providence everything has been entered in advance. And so, prayer becomes the revering of what Providence has foreseen from the beginning. Today confronts eternity. It would be idle to attempt dividing up eternity, introducing finite boundaries into its ever-present now. Such boundaries cannot exist. And so the moment when our questions are answered should be experienced only in the sense of the eternal, patterning ourselves on the eternal Word and partaking in its reality.

If a person brings a concern of his to another, asking him to include it in his prayer, thus giving it enforcement before God, it can be that the one praying is momentarily burdened by that request. But then the matter goes through him and through the sacrament, as it were, and reaches the eternal Word. This passage implies clarification, purification and also a broadening of what is prayed for until it attains proportions pleasing to God. And the one presenting the matter to God can have the experience that the request, as it enters his prayer, suddenly undergoes a transformation and receives an unsuspected meaning and a new content. He will then feel the extent to which such a "bearing of concerns" is grace, since it implies new participation in the life of the sacraments. All individual prayer takes a road leading over the Church's sacramental reality, and here it experiences a transformation. Whoever tries to pray earnestly, with the mind of the Church in the place of others, will experience mysteries touching the sacramental reality which one who merely "receives the sacraments" would perhaps not have noticed.

The sacrament *bestows* by itself *being bestowed*. The priest who dispenses it mediates it by the power of the Holy Spirit which is blowing through him. In a mysterious place in the Church, there takes place the encounter of the yearning faith of the one praying with the Spirit that is both dispensed and also has full participation in this dispensing, since, as Spirit of Christ and of the Church, it blows and gives shape where it will.

The Church, by administering all the sacraments, also administers in them the reality of an *ecclesial time* that unfolds above our earthly time and takes it up into itself—almost incidentally, as it were—in order to open up for it God's eternal time through the mediation of ecclesial time. The Son became founder of the Church within historical time. As he did it, people were able to observe him and believers gathered around him. They stood in their own time as we stand in ours, and they knew the transitory nature of their flesh as much as we. They hardly had an inkling of the fact that, through the Son and his founding of the Church, something permanent was being initiated that was to overcome the passing of time. And yet, this event was for them a revelation of eternal life as much as it is for us. An eternal word is uttered into time; eternal life is poured out over the ephemeral.

Every person knows that his years are numbered and within this limited span of time each individual thing has still more narrowly drawn boundaries. This realization disciplines one into a kind of ascesis of time, an asceticism also practiced outside the Church and consisting in rules of life that each one follows in his own way. The asceticism called for by the following of Christ, however, cannot be derived from such a source. It is an ecclesial and not a worldly ascesis. No one can, at the same time, practice a purely earthly ascesis of time and an ecclesial ascesis of eternity. He must make a clear decision, a decision which an understanding of the sacraments facilitates. Not only have the sacraments been created for the Son; they also contain the shortest road to him and derive directly from him. They are an interchange, to an extent that the things of creation can never be. They constitute a world of their own—the world of the Church—and a time of their own which is eternal time, or, more precisely, the breakthrough of the eternal time into our own time. Through the sacraments, Christian asceticism is loosed from temporality in more than one way, since here every worldly standard, calculation and estimation is bound for failure. Christian asceticism is never brought to a conclusion, nor can a person undertake it only for a limited period of time. One may fast only on certain days, of course, or deprive oneself of a certain amount of sleep only for a period of time. But when the person afterwards again eats and sleeps, mostly because this is the reasonable thing to do, his Christian-ascetical attitude will in no way be compromised. He will, therefore, adopt certain measures for a time, but he will never lay too much store by the deprivations of this period. Grace can transform his appraisal of things, his ability to endure and his power to suffer, either shortening or lengthening them, and he must, for this reason, remain free for this activity of grace and allow it room for play. He will soon realize how real such grace is, and what a preponderant role the sacraments play in it. Signs of this— deafening signs, we might say—are those ascetics whose only nourishment was Holy Communion or those others who hardly ever slept because their apostolate made total claims on their time or others still who undertook the extremest penances, practices that no one else could have endured and which yet, for them, were precisely what was demanded. Behind every Christian ascetic there stands the Cross as total ascesis and total sacrament, and the power of the Cross is mediated through the individual sacraments. The penitential life of Christian ascetics is no adventure into the void, rather strict discipleship in the Church, always including the institutional aspect of the Church. The penances of the saints are mainly to be understood as the Church's response to the gift of priesthood, which is nothing other than a life poured out for the Lord. What, in the sacraments, is a life of ministry by means of the sacraments becomes, in the saints' life of the vows, the subjective response of love. Both things complete one another and come together to form the Church's unified existence and service to the Lord.

In this way, the sacraments endow asceticism with a certain power, a power that spills over from eternity into time. It is something which man cannot imagine on his own, something beyond man's most extreme hopes and which he cannot in any way measure. This power is something greater than man which approximates the Lord's own quality of always being greater than any creature. Just as Christian asceticism as a whole ultimately evades the laws of time on account of its incommensurability, so, too, its particular forms. These cannot be prescribed positively and cannot even be copied adequately after they have come into existence. Asceticism is a permanently living response to a question which the sacraments pose to man.

Between asceticism and the sacraments, therefore, there exists much more than a mere parallel or analogy. A hidden unity connects them which has its source in the Son's act of surrendering his flesh for the world. This surrender exhibits an inseparable double form: a sacramental form in the Eucharist and an ascetical form in the Cross. Neither may be measured by a human standard. For this reason, even in Christian asceticism a concern for (human) standards can never play a determining role. The Lord's suffering does not gradually intensify; in advance it presents him with a pure *excess of demand*. The phase of suffering's "equilibrium", where it would have sufficed, is simply skipped. The feeling of not being able to go any further already dominates the Lord's anguish on the Mount of Olives. A feeling for time is also effaced from the beginning, and at the Cross it is somehow totally superceded. A sort of "timelessness" is here involved which so wholly belongs to eternity that it could not be registered in the experience of the suffering Lord. During this "time" the graves of the dead break open, a sign of the full presence of eternity. The Lord's Passion can find distant analogies in man's natural and supernatural suffering, and this is but one more reason not to reckon with time where asceticism is concerned, just as in the sacraments eternal time becomes a present reality.

At first sight, it would seem we can describe asceticism as the acceptance and performance of a particular task. But the identity of this task is not disclosed. The identity is in God. Acceptance of the task could possibly result in an impulse of generosity that says, "We *will* do it!" With the perseverance required as a basic attitude toward God, however, it will soon become obvious that no genuine asceticism has been present, but that the will had overestimated itself and is now not strong enough to carry out its task. The task is always wholly objective; but grace lies hidden within the objective and it never loses its subjective character, since even the most objective of God's graces is totally personal in what concerns man.

From the standpoint of this insight, we could now describe asceticism as being the precipitation of God's love in man, the attempt on man's part to give an answer to God's perfect love, in order to give over personally to this love what it longs to receive from every person. But with this attempt there is always bound the realization of a total insufficiency and failure. And in every case this awareness is a precipitation of love and a part of the ascetical attitude. Whoever has not reached such an insight will probably practice asceticism as a kind of athletic training, striving toward "championship" and a "perfect record". Christian asceticism can never attain to a goal since it stands in the face of the Perfect. One could surely object that, through asceticism, progress in the spiritual life is attained. This progress may even be described in its various stages, all of which bear a name. Such an objection, however, would totally overlook the essence of asceticism, which consists precisely in *not* weighing and *not* counting, so that the spirit may become perfectly free in the Lord for prayer and its demands. And if asceticism still had to have a goal, it would be more prayer, deeper adoration, greater obedience. Whatever achievement may be attained by genuine asceticism causes no satisfaction, but also little worry. It rather allows a person to strive to stand in peace before God and to remain watchful for his demands. Asceticism is a work of peace, but this peace is not its ultimate goal. It is peaceful in order to give more to God, in order to effect a more profound stripping of the person praying, a more thoroughgoing renunciation of whatever "riches" might be his: in a word, a more earnest disappropriation of the person.

Asceticism's ultimate goal is the poverty of love, poverty on all levels, especially on the spiritual and intellectual level. It is like the love of a physician for his patients, a love that demands of them the strict compliance with difficult prescriptions which have their healing as a goal. In asceticism, convalescence consists in the nearness of God.

A person who leads a difficult life of penance, and who denies himself many things in order to perform this ministry adequately, will surely experience hours of happiness and of God's tangible nearness, hours of warmth in which he is flooded by God's light and which fill him with joy. But these hours are a "surplus gift" of grace. In itself, grace remains austere—not humorless, not without a certain smile—but so austere that a person has to live in intense discipline, in watchfulness and, yet, continually in objective love. When, during his public life, the Lord corrects his Mother, his strictness makes our understanding shrink back, and we would almost ask, "Where has all his love gone?" We then have to consider that the Lord's words in this case are at once an extreme demand and already an answer to his Mother's ascesis. Because she has uttered her consent, she is kept in the discipline in which she herself wants to live, a discipline which lends her existence the spotless form of objectivity. But, if those who do the will of the Lord are "his mother", then, along with the demand for asceticism, there becomes visible at once the perfect fruit that ripens for others. The Son himself distributes the graces that flow forth from his Mother's consent. These graces so wholly belong to him that he has them at his disposal even in the case of his Mother and the answer he gives her, without having to mention the fact that she is the one who mediates the graces. In relation to his preaching to his disciples, Mary is like the ball of Thérèse of Lisieux, which lies hidden and punctured in a corner. She performed *one* service, and now the Son can turn to other things. And yet this comparison is not fully satisfying, since the Mother perseveres in her original readiness, and the Son can at any time draw further fruits from her consent and distribute them, both anticipating her collaboration and in union with her, even at a distance.

Faith bestows on every person who possesses it joys that are founded above all on the triune God and on his Church, and thus no one can say that the Christian ascetic has renounced joy. He has chosen hidden joys which are concealed in God. He has "renounced" only insofar as he knows that the way of asceticism is hard, that he must be blind and deaf in order to follow that way and resist the enticements that arise along its course. But these renunciations are for the sake of arriving at the destination so naked and so bare that God the Father will recognize in this traveler's denudation the likeness of his Son on the Cross, and acknowledge the ascetic's co-meritorious solidarity with the excess of suffering demanded of the Son, the suffering which affected the redemption of the whole world. Here lies the ultimate joy of the penitent.

God loves God to an extent, with a permanence—

indeed, with a *violence*—that we can hardly conceive. Whenever we think we are beginning to grasp this love, we can be sure that it is always much more. Each little sign of it we are capable of perceiving contains in itself infinitely more than we are able to decipher, and even such a sign suffices to excite new and enduring love in countless persons, and to generate a new creation of genuine love in persons who, at best, were lukewarm and for whom the word "love" lacked all content.

Faith mediates to us insights into this love. We perceive them in the Church, in the sacraments, in Scripture. If we consider Scripture attentively, we would see—and adore—the first love blazing up in the most insignificant words. There are moments in prayer when we encounter God's love in such a way that we think we have been finally freed of our lukewarmness and can now give a definitive answer to his love. Then we fall back upon ourselves as if nothing had happened. And yet we know that something *has* happened, and this "something" is nothing less than love, and we know we must foster and bear this love no matter how lukewarm, slothful, and impotent we might be. Because an encounter has taken place, its effects remain, and they compel us to admit that an encounter is to be found even where we are not looking for it; that an encounter always occurs in connection with love; that our everyday life is full of signs of love; and that we are simply too negligent to recognize these signs, to reach out for them, or to make something out of their presence. We must learn to love to the extreme even when we do not *feel* love, and to believe that God listens to every prayer and never turns away, always remaining the same, while it is only *our* perceptions that are dull. Such a trial could be imposed by God, could even be a sign of *his* love, which seeks to make us ever more watchful.

But God has placed in our hands something infinitely precious: love for our neighbor. This love must be continually present to our mind's eye, but not for us to mirror ourselves in and, thus, come to a standstill, choosing it as an object for reflection. We must be aware of this love in order to share it, seeking for those who need it and keeping ourselves from erecting a wall between us and our neighbor, instead letting all pre-existing obstacles tumble to the ground. Our love must not be based on indifference, or take the innocuous form of a general love of "the masses"; it should be the kind of love that considers each individual and concerns itself for him, a love that teaches us how to turn every encounter into an encounter of love, even when the circumstances of the other person—his rejection of us, perhaps—make our task difficult. For love of neighbor is a task that God has entrusted to us so as to make us transparent to God's love, in such a way that our neighbor—whoever he is—will sense what God has intended for him through us: what God has given us to pass on. We can say that our love for God does not have to be excessively subjective; but our love for our neighbor absolutely requires such subjectivity, which we calmly nourish on the objectivity of our love for God.

In his response to this love which has approached him, our neighbor will ask himself from where it is that the power of the one loving him derives, and what it is about it that has both touched and affected him as one loved. He will wonder about the source of this interior radiance. In answering this question—a question which need not be asked explicitly—the person finds his way back to the love of God. Further questions will accost him and make him into a seeker, and "whoever seeks shall find".

Once the person who prays attains to the realization that only love can win the neighbor over, he will also understand that he needs asceticism precisely in the service of this love. Here asceticism implies giving back to God many things that had been considered personal property and "inalienable rights"; it implies becoming deprived of rights and possessions *so as to love better.* A person's moods and preferences must become unimportant to him, so that the whole meaning of his existence and faith may be transferred to the love of neighbor. Only then will he be able to appear before his neighbor as stripped and as undemanding as he must appear before God.

It is not first the neighbor and then God, rather first God and then the neighbor, but in such rapid succession that this "first" and this "then" seem to be indistinguishable. For God loves man not least of all in order to teach him love of neighbor. When the Son pronounces his commandments, he does not do it from the distance, as it were, from a remoteness that has no relationship to man's life. He does it out of his own love for God and man, from his immediate proximity as one of us, as one who speaks to us, as *the* one among us who practices perfect love and who, precisely as a man, was able to appraise exhaustively the hardships surrounding love of neighbor.

The Lord's Mother offers us a model of human asceticism in her encounter with the angel. "Be it done unto me according to your word": with these words she hands her life over to the Holy Spirit, to the Father and to the Son. She knows no further conditions. When we, as believers, hear what the remainder of her life consisted of, we witness a stream of hardships: the hardships of the Nativity, until she found a stable in which to give birth; the hardships of the flight into Egypt; the hardships, also, that the Son brought her on account of his mission. But what radiates out of all the hardships of this life is her victory, a victory through self-denial and asceticism. Never does she think of herself: in all she does she remains open to her Son's needs, and, in her woman's way, she smooths out the road before him as best she can. For the rest, she accompanies him on his way to death, both understanding and not understanding the reasons for it—in the spirit of true obedience, therefore—in order to carry out the things he has entrusted to her even when he disappears from her sight. This is asceticism in the highest sense of discipleship, given to all of us as an example. In this process, she does not remain alone. We see her united to Joseph, to John the Evangelist and to all others she encounters. We also know that her asceticism derives directly from the Son's own love and the substance of his life. She deeply venerates this love and keeps her gaze fixed on it, and this veneration of the Son in no way curtails her adoration of the Father and the Spirit. She perseveres before the face of the triune God, in the expectation of what the Word might demand, in the carrying out of all the tasks indicated to her, in the humble extinction of self that asceticism ultimately demands from every person. She fully actualizes the unity of love and asceticism. Here, both the concept and the word "asceticism" can recede into the background, since its content has now been fully taken over by love. The same thing is true of the Son. With him, too, asceticism no longer appears to be an activity and a "subject" with a standing of its own. In its every aspect, the Son's "asceticism" dissolves into his love, which alone sheds its light over the whole of his life: his love for us, his love for the Father, both his heavenly love and that other love which invites John to lean on his breast at the moment when he distributes himself in the form of bread and wine. We then understand that our ascetical efforts must exhibit the traces of this love to such an extent that in our case, too, no one can speak of *us,* but of *love.* This is an all-conquering love, and it conquers even the praying believer so perfectly that whoever sees him experiences only love and its resplendent victory. It conquers so thoroughly that the "scaffolding" of Cross and suffering are now removed and we can see nothing other than God's love for his redeemed world.